WOMEN *on the* BALLOT

PATHWAYS TO POLITICAL POWER

PLUMLEAF PRESS

An Imprint of Rubicon Publishing Inc.

www.plumleafpress.com | www.rubiconpublishing.com

Associate Publisher: Amy Land
Executive Editor: Teresa Carleton
Editor: Stephanie Rotz
Creative Director: Jennifer Drew
Designers: Robin Forsyth, Jason Mitchell

Funded by the
Government
of Canada | Canada

19 20 21 22 23   5 4 3 2 1

ISBN 978-1-4869-3269-6

Printed in China

August, 2019

BETSY McGREGOR

WOMEN
on the
BALLOT

PATHWAYS TO POLITICAL POWER 🍁

Dr. Betsy McGregor

TRIBUTE & DEDICATION

This labour of love is in tribute to my mother, Eileen Stevenson McGregor, who dreamed, dared, and did. Her kindness, indomitable spirit, empowering optimism, and adventurous energy imprinted itself on me and was a gift in countless other women's lives. This book is also in tribute to my father's gentleness and integrity.

I am dedicating *Women on the Ballot* to my two treasured granddaughters, Mae Elizabeth and Lauren Eileen, and to all the young girls in their generation around the world. I trust you girls will seize leadership, in all its forms, and confidently design a vibrant, peace-driven future for us all. Never doubt your ability or your vision.

Finally, this book came into being because of my son's uplifting inspiration in my life, love, and rock-solid support. For all the adventures we have shared and more to come, Mac, this book is for you with love and admiration from your mom.

Contents

PREFACE..10

PREAMBLE 12

Part 1   ASSESSING THE JOURNEY

Changing the Political Landscape........................ 17

That's It — I'm Running! 26

Starting Points 37

Politics and Identity 43

Never Doubt Yourself 52

Run, Ask, or Support 56

Part 2   WHAT DOES IT TAKE?

Training, Networks, and Mentors......................... 67

Getting on the Ballot 75

The Campaign Trail... 86

Running for Leadership 100

Part 3   HOW TO SURVIVE — AND THRIVE

Managing the Message 117

Finding the Money..139

Age Is Overrated 139

Complex Trade-Offs 144

New Directions...158

Part 4   A WORLD MADE ANEW

Making Herstory Visible 175

Feminism and Politics 184

Creating Enduring Change...193

More Than Just Numbers 201

POSTSCRIPT 214

ACKNOWLEDGEMENTS 216

APPENDIX 218

REFERENCES 237

INDEX 243

PREFACE

On the day my mother turned 10 years old, 18 October 1929, women were recognized constitutionally as "persons" in Canada. It took until my mother was 41 for every woman in Canada to win the right to vote. That was in 1960. Fast-forward almost 60 years to 2019. Women have won barely 27 percent of the seats in Canada's House of Commons.

The goal of this book is to equip and empower women to run for political office. *Women on the Ballot* tells the stories of more than 90 women in politics in Canada. Each is a trailblazer. Among these women are 37 members of Parliament, 21 members of provincial or territorial legislatures, 4 Indigenous leaders, 6 mayors, 4 federal party leaders, 2 premiers, and 1 prime minister.

The youngest woman in this book became Chief at 23. The oldest, a runner-up for World Mayor in 2005, served 36 years as mayor before retiring from politics at the age of 93. The women interviewed come from very different backgrounds, races, ethnicities, sexual orientations, classes, and religions. From across Canada, at all levels of politics and from all parties,

including First Nations governance, they chose to lead.

With my tape recorder in hand, I spoke with these women. My own story in politics was the thread that wove the tales together. I felt overwhelmed by the desire to give back, emotional about so many of their stories, and honoured that these women were so willing to share tales of their heights and depths. Each woman gave different reasons to explain why she had run for political office. Most said they were driven to action by issues they knew they could affect if they had power. As one woman said, "It's the issues that keep you awake at night." From practical tips to unexpected insights, hard-earned lessons to humorous encounters, these women share glimpses of their struggles and triumphs and, in doing so, reveal a good deal about us as Canadians. Some succeeded beyond all imagination. Others vanished at the first and hardest hurdle, the nomination. Many bottomed out and then climbed out to run again or to move on with grace. It's not all pretty. It's greater than grit. It's as tough as the women themselves.

Writing this book was a three-year journey. I wrote at the lake, on the shores of Normandy, in Paris, France, and at Trent University, where the Planet café kept me fed, the gym kept me fit, and the voices of the women kept me company. The power of the stories kept me going. I remain moved by the women's dedication to public service.

This book began on the day I decided not to run for election in 2015. I had been a nomination candidate three times and a federal candidate twice, in 2008 and again in 2011. I loved it. Even though circumstances precluded my taking a third run, it was difficult not to be on the ballot. Making the decision not to run spurred me on to make "being on the ballot" happen for as many other women in Canada as possible by running nomination battles, teaching leadership in schools, staying engaged at the Harvard Kennedy School, running campaign schools, and writing this book.

Like all great adventures in life, especially daunting ones driven by great purpose, starting is the toughest step. Self-doubt can delay putting oneself out there. So, *Women on the Ballot* begins by exploring *why* — why risk it all? It then turns to *how*. It demystifies the political process. The trailblazers in this book tell tales of the accelerators, brakes, detours, and ditches they encountered along the way. Their stories of money, the media, mentors, and mothers are fascinating and inspiring.

Leaving politics at any stage of the journey is as challenging as deciding to enter politics in the first place. Women in this book are examples of the strength and courage needed to run, win or lose, and then move on.

At current rates, reaching gender parity in politics will take another 100 years. A great deal needs to change. The first step is for more women to run. Canada needs more women in political power. The women in this book have helped shine a light on the path — the premise is that if you can see her, you can be her. It's time for the women of today and tomorrow to read the colourful stories in *Women on the Ballot*, seize the lessons learned, and then pick up the torch and run. It is time to dare to be inspirational. That is my dream for you.

— *Betsy McGregor*

PREAMBLE

In the early part of the 20th century, women in Canada did not legally qualify as "persons" under the British North America Act of 1867, now known as the Constitution Act, and therefore they could not be appointed to the Senate. Five fearless women from Alberta disagreed with this. They filed a petition in Canada's Supreme Court on 27 August 1927. The Court decided unanimously against them. Undaunted, they appealed to the Judicial Committee of Britain's Privy Council. In what is now termed the Persons Case, they won the appeal in 1929. Women were now legally considered "persons." One year later, in 1930, Cairine Wilson was the first woman to be appointed to the Senate of Canada.

Women's suffrage was another matter. Winning the right to vote did not come easily or all at once. Under Canada's federal electoral law, "idiots, mad men, criminals" and women were not permitted to vote. There were a few exceptions.

Municipalities had taken the lead in getting women the right to vote. By 1900, property-holding women won the earliest victories for the right to vote and to run for city council, which included the right to run in library and school board elections. Provincially, suffragists fought and eventually won voting rights across the country in stages:

Manitoba, Saskatchewan, Alberta (1916), BC and Ontario (1917), Nova Scotia (1918), New Brunswick and Yukon (1919), PEI (1922), Newfoundland and Labrador (1925), Quebec (1940), and the Northwest Territories (1951).

Federally, during the First World War, under the Wartime Elections Act, women who were "British subjects, otherwise qualified as to age, race, and residence, and the wife, widow, mother, sister, or daughter of any person in the naval forces" were permitted to vote. Under the Military Voters Act, women in the military also had the vote.

By 1918, women over 21 who were "not excluded under racial or Indigenous prohibitions" were granted the vote federally. But it wasn't until 1960 that all Canadian women were granted the right to vote nationally. The exclusion of Asian Canadians ended in 1948 and the exclusion of Inuit in 1950 (but ballot boxes weren't brought into Inuit communities until 1962). After the introduction of the Indian Act in 1867, Indigenous women were barred from participating in Band Councils until an amendment to the act in 1951. The right to vote federally was extended to all Indigenous people in 1960. In 1921, Agnes Macphail ran in Alberta for the Progressive Party, a farmer-based party, becoming the first woman to win a seat in Canada's House of Commons.

A bronze sculpture of the "Famous Five," on the grounds of the Manitoba Legislative Building in Winnipeg

As of 1 January 2019, women held 90 of the 334 seats in the House of Commons, making up just under 27 percent, which ranks Canada 62nd globally in the representation of women in government. Yet women may be disproportionately affected by decisions made by the government, including employment, the environment, healthcare, transportation, infrastructure, and immigration. Parity is important and equality undeniably so. But beyond numbers, it is critical that women participate meaningfully in all aspects of the political process. Women's representation matters to democracy.

When women are equally represented in all areas of political life, they can have a positive impact on society and the state of democracy. *Women on the Ballot* taps into trailblazers' advice for beginning the journey, resources to acquire essential skills, strategies for surviving and thriving — and insights on rebounding when it ends. Above all, it points to the power of women in politics to shape the world anew.

Part 1

ASSESSING THE
JOURNEY

W omen are beginning to change the political landscape in Canada. In increasing numbers, they are entering politics at all levels of government. As I contemplated this fact, I wondered what motivated them and began my research. In my interviews with more than 90 women, I began by asking the women if politics had been their life dream. Few felt the word "dream" fit; purpose not position drove them into politics. They were intent on doing something rather than being someone. The sparks that ignited each woman were different, but all were compelling.

This section, "Assessing the Journey," explores the motivations and values that underpinned their decision to enter politics — and some of the things that gave them pause. While the women profiled in this section are changing the political landscape in Canada, women are still under-represented in politics. For example, women are 50 percent of the population, but in the 2015 federal election, they were just under 27 percent of the MPs elected. Compared to 1921, of course, where only one woman, out of a total of 235 total seats, was elected, this is progress. But we can do much more.

The women in this section describe why they ran and how they felt about it — and what helped them decide to enter electoral politics in the first place. Some women describe the barriers that they faced, not only because of their race, ethnicity, religion, or sexual orientation, but also because of their own doubts about their ability. While the decision to take the plunge was not made lightly, it was made, and these women were changed — as was our country.

Women premiers from 2008
to 2019 (from top to bottom):
Eva Aariak, Kathy Dunderdale,
Christy Clark, Alison Redford,
Pauline Marois, Kathleen
Wynne, Rachel Notley

Changing the Political Landscape

The gender gap in power and politics is still wide in Canada. While there are signs of hope, progress toward gender parity is slow and uneven.

From 2008 to 2019, a new high-water mark was reached for women in political leadership in Canada. Seven women served as premiers: Eva Aariak in Nunavut, Kathy Dunderdale in Newfoundland and Labrador, Christy Clark in British Columbia, Alison Redford in Alberta, Pauline Marois in Quebec, Kathleen Wynne in Ontario, and Rachel Notley in Alberta. At this point, the majority of Canadians were living in provinces or territories led by women. By April 2019, not one of these women remained as premier. I wanted to find out why this was — and how we could encourage more women to put their names on the ballot.

There are many firsts among the trailblazers in this book, including the first woman to lead a political party in Canada, Canada's first gay premier, and the first Black woman MP; their arrival ushers in change. With being the first comes a burden of responsibility. People who are the first are often seen as role models and advocates for those who follow. There is the expectation that "things will be different now." In 1975, Bette Stephenson was elected to the Legislative Assembly of Ontario and broke many gender barriers during the 12 years she was in Parliament as the first woman to serve in multiple cabinet positions and as Deputy Premier. But it takes decades to change the culture, and change doesn't come easily. Despite the example set by Stephenson, Ontario didn't have its first woman premier until 2013.

What does it take to change history? Kim Campbell helped shape a new normal for women in politics in Canada when, in 1993, she became Canada's first woman prime minister. She has courage, intellect, and tenacity. It takes many such trailblazers to change the political landscape.

Official portrait of Kim Campbell — the first and only woman prime minister of Canada to date

KIM CAMPBELL

Lawyer, diplomat, author, and teacher, Kim Campbell ran for politics at all three levels and served as Canada's 19th prime minister from June 1993 to November 1993. Previously, Campbell had also been Canada's first woman Minister of Justice, Attorney General, and Minister of Defence.

I remember the night of the leadership convention. One of my supporters had tears rolling down his cheeks. "This is for my daughter," he said. He was very aware of what had just happened. He knew what a departure it was. I don't think I was shocked. Exhausted, exhilarated, yes. It was the same me, but things had changed. They would never be the same again. It was almost too much to take in. The leadership campaign was something you put so much of yourself into it. You pumped so much adrenaline. Then, it washes over you. The reality sinks in. I was going to be prime minister. The first female prime minister of Canada. It was a wonderful feeling. I have been on the other side when that enormous push of adrenaline ends in defeat. I know how hard it is to take that in too.

> *The reality sinks in. I was going to be prime minister. The first female prime minister of Canada.*

I was aware of how high the stakes were. I also knew how hard it was going to be and how much there was to do. But I really did try to allow myself to savour it. And I think that's important. To permit yourself that moment to say, "Yes. It happened!" I had been elected leader of my party the night before. That meant that I would be sworn in as Canada's prime minister.

It was going to mean a lot to a lot of people. To be the vehicle of that landmark is really rewarding. Truly humbling. But what did it feel like that next morning when the realization hit me? It was quite wonderful. It was a thrill.

CELINA CAESAR-CHAVANNES

Celina Caesar-Chavannes's successful campaign for Liberal MP in 2015 led to her becoming appointed as parliamentary secretary to the prime minister and later parliamentary secretary to the Minister of International Development. She left the Liberal caucus in March 2019 to sit as an Independent.

At the signing ceremony for new members of Parliament (MPs) on Parliament Hill, when the clerk said, "You, like everyone else before you, are about to sign your name into history," everything set in — the weight of it all. My uncle Norman, patriarch of the family and an invited guest to this ceremony, said, "Look at you. This little Black girl from back home in Grenada signing your name into history below the biggest picture of the Fathers of Confederation I have ever seen." The contrast was not lost on me.

Much lies ahead, but I am prepared to be among those courageous path-breakers confronting racism and lifting our common sights in Canadian politics to be fully inclusive of women of colour. Breaking the racial barrier carries challenges. Remarkable Black women in politics have come before me in provincial legislatures and the House of Commons — and Canada has also been served by Michaëlle Jean, our first Black governor general. We are very visible, but we are the exception. It can be very lonely.

I draw strength every time I walk past Kim Campbell's portrait in Centre Block. She is our first and, so far, only female prime minister. Everyone who visits our Parliament Buildings sees her image as prime minister. Now that's sending signals. I inhale her energy each time I see her.

> *I draw strength every time I walk past Kim Campbell's portrait in Centre Block.*

NAHANNI FONTAINE

Nahanni Fontaine was elected as the MLA for St. Johns in Manitoba in 2016 and became NDP House Leader of the Official Opposition in 2019. She is Ojibway from the Sagkeeng Anishinaabe First Nation in southern Manitoba.

Let me talk about the space — the legislature space, I mean. Every legislator elected can sit in that space. You cannot go in that space unless you're an elected member, a page, a clerk, or the Speaker. No one in the public gets to go into that space. It is one of the most privileged spaces we have in Canada.

I want to share a story with you. I was thinking that these spaces were not meant for people like me. When we first went to take our seats in the legislature, with the Speech from the Throne, it didn't seem real. I felt that Indigenous people were never meant to be there. Women were never meant to be there. Imagine sitting in this space. My childhood as an Indigenous woman welled up inside me. Then I started to notice that I was crying after Question Periods. I noticed I was angry and depressed. I went for long walks with my dog, and I realized that I was mourning the life that I had lived and the work that I was doing before politics. The change was difficult emotionally and spiritually. Before politics, I was doing such profound work with families of the Missing and Murdered Indigenous Girls and Women. It was so purposeful. It gave me meaning.

Suddenly there I was, sitting in the legislature. It is a profoundly white male space. I was quite affronted by the heckling — constant heckling. From an Indigenous perspective, culturally, we just do not do that. You see it on TV, but when you're in it, it is so toxic. You can literally feel the toxicity. You breathe in white male privilege. You breathe it in when the

"
I was thinking that these spaces were not meant for people like me.

premier is making a cut of $120,000 on one of the most marginalized, poorest neighbourhoods that Indigenous people are living in. Your spirit and emotions get assaulted. I had to figure out how to navigate through this space. I developed strategies to emotionally and spiritually protect myself. I always stared at the Speaker. I never looked at the other side. It was a shield. When I was first elected, I made a commitment to Creator that I would never heckle. I made this promise not just to Creator but to myself. It was beneath me as an Indigenous woman. If you ever choose to run, the first day that you sit in that house, you'll know exactly what I mean when I speak about the spirit of that space.

We are celebrating women firsts in public life.

LINDA REID

First elected in 1991 as a member of the Liberal caucus and re-elected seven consecutive times, Linda Reid set a record, becoming the longest-serving woman in the British Columbia Legislative Assembly.

When I arrived in 1991 [as an MLA], I could not find a single picture of a female legislator. The walls were adorned with older, Caucasian men in power. So, I set about creating a permanent display of all the women firsts in our province. We call it "One Hundred Years of Women and the Vote." The wall displays our first female elected, first Korean Canadian, first Japanese Canadian, first female Speaker, premier, and lieutenant governor. We are celebrating women firsts in public life. I want every girl who comes on tour with her Grade 5 class to see women's pictures and be inspired. I want them to see their own image and know they belong in the legislature. Today there is a British Columbia Youth Parliament. It used to be the Older Boys' Parliament of BC. We had to fight to open it to girls. It is truly an amazing organization. It takes high school students and has them sit in the legislature between Christmas and New Year and pass legislation. They learn the process and then take projects back to their schools. We have a responsibility to teach kids how to give back to their communities, and girls must share this chance equally.

FARHEEN KHAN

In 2015, Farheen Khan took the federal NDP nomination in the riding of Mississauga Centre in Ontario. She was the only hijab-wearing woman to run during the election campaign.

I understood from the outset that I was bringing unique attributes to the party. I was a Muslim woman who also wore a hijab. Had I been elected, I would have represented a first for women. It came as no surprise that my image was used on brochures as emblematic of the party's outreach and commitment to diversify its candidates. I also knew I would be the brunt of expressions of discrimination. I understood my advantage and accepted the realities I would face as part of the risk-benefit equation. I believe that parties need to prepare newer candidates of diverse backgrounds more completely for debates and responses at doors. The desire for change defines many election outcomes. Some candidates, supported in part for their diversity characteristics, achieve unparalleled opportunities once elected. They are a mark of this moment in time and the transition toward diversity. But some change agents pay a price challenging traditional power structures. These women are in the front lines at the doors and in debates. Not all win. But all open the way for broader understanding.

> *Some change agents pay a price challenging traditional power structures.*

JEAN AUGUSTINE

Jean Augustine was the first Black woman to be elected to the House of Commons in 1993 and, in 2002, with her cabinet appointment as Minister of State (Multiculturalism and Status of Women), became the first Black woman appointed to cabinet. She served as an MP for the Liberal Party for four terms until her retirement in 2005.

Racism was never raised at the doors when I canvassed. All-candidates debates were driven by issues and were respectful. I was never attacked as a woman, a Black, Catholic, or immigrant. Two things did tag me at the outset. I lived blocks outside the riding, and I was appointed as the candidate. I fought hard to earn every vote. I was told after my first race that I had earned more of the women's vote than any other candidate across the country. I ran four times — 1993, 1997, 2000, and 2004. Despite all the contributions to Canada that Blacks had been making since 1604, only two Black men had ever made it to the House before 1993. No woman ever had.

The moment I walked down the Parliament Building hall and into the House of Commons, I was in awe. I felt a deep sense of history, the honour, and the responsibility. I knew every Black person would be watching. One funny thing happened which reflected the amount of hope pinned on me being in the "first wave" of Black members of Parliament. It arrived by post. A man in jail had written, saying, "Now that you're an MP, can you get me out of jail?" Expectations were rather distorted. In seriousness, the moment provided a signal that the door was now open. "You can do it!"

> *I felt a deep sense of history, the honour, and the responsibility. I knew every Black person would be watching.*

That's It — I'm Running!

The principles of democracy must be continuously defended. Many of the women in this book began a career in politics to fight for fairness. In their view, the issues that engaged them, their life experience expertise, and other intersections of identity were not adequately represented in the people, policies, and priorities they saw at political decision tables. Democracy is not a spectator sport. These women shared a similar sense of urgency and a readiness to act. Their purpose grounded them when things became difficult and helped them rebound when it was all over.

The specific sparks that ignited their decision to enter politics were very different. For some, the catalyst that set things in motion was the power of a single conversation. For others, a passion for politics arose from their own familial and personal circumstances. After a career wrestling with issues in development, gender, science, and ethics, I, too, wanted to be part of the decision-making. Living an issue first-hand gives you a powerful focus forged in fire; these are sparks that can't be extinguished. The trailblazers in this section share the fire that fuelled their readiness to act.

I saw a direct role for government in helping people like my brother achieve their full potential.

PEGGY SATTLER

A lifelong advocate for Canadians with disabilities, Peggy Sattler was elected as an MPP for the Ontario NDP in 2013. Previously, Sattler served as a trustee on the Thames Valley District School Board for 13 years, including two terms as board chair.

I am the eldest daughter of an immigrant working-class family. I have a younger brother with an intellectual disability. There was no special education in Ontario at the time. My mother became a fierce advocate to get him access to the educational supports he needed. He ended up going to what was then called "a school for the trainably retarded."

I volunteered at his school. His disability was formative for me. I saw first-hand how people treated my brother differently. I knew his life chances were going to be limited. It also taught me the power of advocacy and planted in me, from an early age, the seeds of social justice. Certain roles in life are predetermined by chance and circumstance. That seemed profoundly unfair to me. I saw a direct role for government in helping people like my brother achieve their full potential. I wanted to have an impact on this issue.

A new world opened to me when I met Marion Dewar running in a federal by-election for the NDP. I was enthralled by her and energized when I heard her speak. I worked tirelessly on her campaign. When she won, she offered me a position in her office on Parliament Hill. My path into politics had begun.

INDIRA NAIDOO-HARRIS

Indira Naidoo-Harris was born and spent her early years in South Africa under apartheid. Elected as an MPP in 2014 for the Ontario Liberal Party, for Naidoo-Harris, entering politics was a moral imperative.

I felt compelled to run. It was, in the end, my responsibility.

Politics was not something I planned to do. It was a passage that opened along the way. I felt compelled to do it. I have lived under apartheid. In South Africa, I knew first-hand what it meant to have no political voice. When my family immigrated to Canada, they gave up everything to give their children a chance.

I grew up in Canada understanding what a magical and amazing opportunity politics is for a citizen. I felt compelled to run. It was, in the end, my responsibility. My path took me first into journalism. I became a recognizable voice on the ground in the community. I lived in the community where I was running for close to 20 years. I was a hockey mom and soccer mom. From journalism, covering the issues, it was a natural next step to enter politics and seek a place at the decision table.

CHERI DINOVO

During her 11 years as an MPP for Parkdale-High Park in Toronto for the Ontario NDP, Cheri DiNovo passed more private members' bills than any other MPP in Ontario and more pro-LGBTQ2+ legislation than anyone in Canadian history.

In the early 1990s, my husband died in a traffic accident. It was quite traumatizing. I really needed to do something different. So, as a single mom, I went back to school to get my master's in theology. This led to my ordination in the United Church. I was sent to a rural parish to start, then to a city parish.

Two women wanted to be married. I didn't see a reason why they shouldn't be married. I have always been in favour and been active in LGBTQ politics since 1971. The forms we used said bride and groom. I considered it an action of the Holy Spirit that the clerk at the registrar's office thought that one of their names was a man's. It turned out to be the first legalized same-sex marriage in Canada. I subsequently wrote a book, *Qu(e)erying Evangelism*. The path to politics and back again to the ministry took several twists and turns. I was always political, just not always inside politics.

JENNY KWAN

In 1993, Jenny Kwan was elected as a city councillor in Vancouver, becoming the youngest in the city's history. Three years later, she was elected as an MLA for the BC NDP and held a number of cabinet posts; in 2015, she was elected as an MP for the NDP.

It's the issues that keep you awake at night. They will motivate you to overcome your doubts if you are hesitating. You need to love what you do. The rest is easy. I was working as a community legal advocate. My first case was one that would change my life. She was a young refugee who had arrived in Canada with the only other surviving family member, her disabled dad. She was in high school, and her dream was to become a nurse. When she turned 18, the government of the day threatened to cancel her income assistance. It made me so mad because I firmly believe that everyone deserves the chance to succeed. I had lived the immigrant reality. Mothers looked to me as a symbol of what is possible for their daughters. I knew I had the power to give voice to those without a voice. I decided to enter politics and bring that voice to the policy table. Whatever political beliefs you have, base them on your values. You need to believe strongly in them. You need to be passionate about what you believe in.

MORGANE OGER

Before running as an NDP candidate in the 2017 BC provincial election, Morgane Oger was a member of the City of Vancouver's LGBTQ2+ advisory committee and chair of the Trans Alliance Society.

People should be a part of the decision-making about themselves.

I've done a lot of human rights and education activism. Way back, I did direct action for women's equality in Afghanistan. After that, I became involved in the Vancouver School Board. That was a solid decade before I became involved in transgender politics.

A key motivation for me was being painfully aware that on many debates on inclusion and diversity both in Canada and internationally, discussions were being held by non-transgender persons. We were never ever a voice at the table.

There was a time when transgender people were considered to have a mental illness. I wanted to tear that barrier down. I had attended a non-partisan policy workshop held by the United Way of the Lower Mainland. It was pivotal for me. There I met many political figures and began to assess the possibility of running politically.

Entering politics was a challenging route to take, and one I knew would carry a high personal cost. I just wanted to tear that barrier down. People should be a part of the decision-making about themselves.

HAZEL MCCALLION

"Hurricane Hazel" McCallion was elected deputy reeve of Streetsville in 1968, appointed reeve, and then elected mayor in 1970. In 1978, she was elected mayor of Mississauga, and today holds the record as Mississauga's longest-serving mayor (36 years) and is one of the longest-serving mayors in Canada.

I love service. Politics is about people, relationships, and service. There is no such thing as doing it alone. In politics, you deal directly with people. You are a servant of your community. You have to love people and love service. It is all-consuming and all the time. I was 93 when I retired from politics [in 2014]. I never would have been good at provincial or federal politics. I might have found myself in Opposition and certainly compelled to vote against my party and with my conscience.

The Mississauga train derailment of 1979, also known as the Mississauga Miracle, happened almost immediately after my election. Not a single life was lost. I grounded my actions, and all future council decisions, on three principles: first, gather all known facts; second, ensure transparency and clear communications; and finally, always put people first.

Underpinning it all was my terrific team. Politics is not an individual sport. I miss the team!

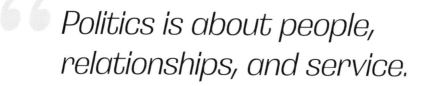

Politics is about people, relationships, and service.

> *Politics is a powerful avenue to preserve and protect language and culture.*

EVA AARIAK

In 1999, Eva Aariak became Nunavut's first languages commissioner and helped lay the groundwork for the Official Languages Act and Inuit Language Protection Act. In 2008, Aariak won a seat for Iqaluit East in the Legislative Assembly of Nunavut and became its first woman premier later that year.

I have always been involved in politics at the community level fighting for the preservation of the culture and language of Inuit. That has always been an important issue for me and the community.

Nunavut is a unique place. The territory has a consensus government. We do not have political parties. We negotiate through communication and dialogue. Some of Canada may not know that about the North.

My involvement in community radio and TV helped equip me for entering politics. The urgent need to protect our culture and language was always present. When I eventually entered politics, I was honoured and humbled to be chosen to be premier.

Politics is a powerful avenue to preserve and protect language and culture. It was one that enabled me to advance and promote the preservation of culture, language, and customs of Inuit.

> *At the soul of leadership is love of your people and deep commitment to community service.*

PHYLLIS WILLIAMS

Phyllis Williams grew up in a family committed to community leadership. In 2012, she became the second woman to be elected Chief of Curve Lake First Nation.

At the soul of leadership is love of your people and deep commitment to community service.

My grandmother was my first role model because she, at the time, became the first woman councillor when Elsie Knott became the first female Chief in all of Canada. My grandmother Adeline was

Elsie's aunt and accomplished the Head Council seat, defeating several men. This was the first time when women could run. These two risk-taking women demonstrated they could run households, care for children, and represent community politics.

In Elsie's political career and as an entrepreneur, she demonstrated that the business and political world could be led by women. She excelled at both. I also had two male cousins who became Chief, so service was deeply rooted in our family. I knew what service to the community involved. I also served as a volunteer on several committees of council previously and was elected to council for 16 years prior to becoming Chief.

Our community is on a peninsula between Buckhorn and Chemong Lakes, which can be challenging for economic development and needed infrastructure. Clean water, education, health, and housing are important issues alongside preservation of our culture and language.

Our Curve Lake community has also among us victims of residential schools and the Sixties Scoop. Canada's Truth and Reconciliation Commission report "Honouring the Truth, Reconciling for the Future" contains 94 Calls to Action. As leaders, we are responsible to implement this roadmap with all Canadians.

BARDISH CHAGGER

Her father's involvement with local politics was the spark that ignited Bardish Chagger's passion for politics. She ran in the 2015 federal election for the Liberal Party and won, going on to become Canada's first woman House Leader.

The government of the day didn't represent my idea of Canadian values, so I took up the challenge, stepped into politics, and never looked back.

I am a child of immigrants. It was as if two worlds were colliding. At school in Canada, we were encouraged to develop strong opinions and raise questions, but at home, culturally, that didn't fly. At home, I was the second of six children, challenging my father and pushing boundaries. This was far from traditional custom in India.

My father welcomed it, but I am not sure, at the outset, his views were entirely shared by my grandparents. It took lots of flexibility exercised by everyone to bridge the two worlds as I entered full force into my passion for federal politics.

The government of the day didn't represent my idea of Canadian values, so I took up the challenge, stepped into politics, and never looked back. My family remains my pillar. I admire so deeply their collective courage to bridge different worlds and mingle diverse cultures. After all, that's our Canada.

> I entered politics full force as the most effective channel for change.

ELIZABETH MAY

An environmentalist, activist, and lawyer, as well as the author of eight books, Green Party Leader Elizabeth May was the first member of the Green Party to win a seat in the House of Commons.

For me, it has always been about being effective. I was asked to run by NDP leaders Audrey McLaughlin, Alexa McDonough, and Jack Layton, Liberal leaders Sheila Copps, Jean Chrétien, and Paul Martin, and even by Progressive Conservative Joe Clark. I took their invitations very seriously. I always ended up deciding that it was more useful to keep working as a non-partisan in the environmental movement.

In the mid-1980s, I was an environmental lawyer in the environment minister's office for the Progressive Conservatives, though I never was a party member. I gained great familiarity with the political process but also watched MPs and ministers not be able to accomplish their goals. Constrained by political realities, they were not heard. I decided to take a job with the [environmental non-profit] Sierra Club. My decisions to say no to politics over many decades had more to do with assessing my ability to be effective.

This same reason drove me into politics. In November 2005, I watched with great distress as the NDP and Conservatives brought down the Liberal government, and Mr. Harper became prime minister. I knew him well from fighting on the front lines of climate change. It was a heartbreaker for me. I knew we were in for a very rough road. Effectiveness for me is always the deciding factor. I knew that under Mr. Harper, the non-partisan globalization of public support for climate action was going to fall on deaf ears. I knew the writing was on the wall for charity organizations championing climate change.

Calls quickly came from friends in the Green Party across Canada. One of my models was Germany's Green Party Leader Petra Kelly. I could see her impact in politics. I took out a Green Party membership and entered the political fray of a competitive leadership race. There was no turning back. I entered politics full force as the most effective channel for change.

AMANDA LATHLIN

In a by-election in 2015, Amanda Lathlin, born and raised in Opaskwayak Cree Nation, was the first First Nations woman elected to the Manitoba Legislature. She is a member of the NDP caucus.

In the beginning, I never imagined she would be my inspiration. Her name was Helen Betty Osborne. She was only 19 at the time [when she was murdered]. A lot of people knew who her murderers were. No one really came forward because she was an Aboriginal girl and people were too scared to come forward.

All the racism I had experienced in school rushed to the surface. The disregard for her kidnapping and death diminished how I looked at myself. It impacted my self-esteem as an Aboriginal girl. I belonged to a group of people who could be discarded and forgotten and not cared about. My great-grandmother, grandmothers, and mother all went to residential schools. Low self-esteem was instilled and perpetuated across three generations. It was intergenerational.

I grew up in a single-parent family living in social housing. I always thought I could not go beyond the fences of social housing. An important moment happened when I was in Grade 4. My mother sent me to a summer program at the school gymnasium. I met two Cree women who were leaders of the school program. It was the first time I ever saw Aboriginal women leaders. I asked them how they ever got there. It had a profound impact on me. They explained they were university students studying to become schoolteachers. That floored me. I never knew that was possible.

I was so determined to go to university. They became role models. They still have an impact on me to this day. I spoke about them in my maiden speech in the legislature when I was sworn in.

In elementary school, we had only learned about the Métis, the fur trade, and voyageurs. There was nothing about my own real history. At university, I finally learned my own history and started to appreciate my own roots. I learned about Aboriginal political movements, Treaty rights, and Supreme Court cases. A pride arose within me. My self-esteem arose through education.

With the position I now hold as MLA, I have the right to express and address these issues on the floor of the legislature. Entering politics was not easy, but it gave me a path and a voice to help others.

Entering politics was not easy, but it gave me a path and a voice to help others.

It is important to speak your truth in the legislature. My daughters, Elyse and Natanis, have been flown to Winnipeg and Brandon for self-harm and suicide attempts. Sitting in emergency all night [in Winnipeg with one daughter], all I felt was the role of a frightened struggling mother, not an MLA. All I could think of was all the parents that were in the same situation with fewer hands to reach for help. I admired my daughter's courage to heal. In the end, it was her hand holding my hand. I spoke on the floor of the legislature about her and all the contributing factors that led to these realities. Now, my number-one issue is to be an advocate for mental health for youth.

I never dreamt that one day I would be elected as the first Aboriginal female MLA in the history of Manitoba. The story of Helen Betty Osborne deflated me when I was young. I accepted I was going to live with racism and discrimination. After being elected in the same constituency where she lived in my hometown, I never thought I would represent the riding where this tragedy happened — where she lived and was murdered. They still have memorial walks for her. I met with her family for a powerful moment on her walk last summer. We stood on the spot where Helen Betty was murdered and said prayers for her.

Starting Points

Women from diverse professional and social backgrounds bring a wide range of skills to public office and add unique perspectives to discussions and debates. Political decisions touch every aspect of our lives, including our access, equitable or inequitable, to social services, healthcare, education, infrastructure, and justice. Public policy decisions benefit from robust debates — women's voices must be present in decisions that have an impact on our communities and on our international relations.

Unlike many fields, there is no one background required to apply for the position. For example, my background was in veterinary medicine and work with the UN. From rural to urban spaces, First Nations to new Canadians, and corporate boardrooms to community organizations, varied experiences add important value and depth to debates at Canada's political decision-making tables.

LIBBY DAVIES

Libby Davies, MP from 1997 to 2015 for the NDP and a city councillor from 1982 to 1993, was a familiar sight on the steps of city hall and the provincial legislature as a well-known community activist.

These were not hypothetical policy debates. ... We were working on life and death issues.

When I was 19 years old, I started working as a Downtown Eastside organizer [in Vancouver]. It just took me over. People were dying in fires and living in slum housing with horrible landlords. People had no heat and lived in terrible conditions.

For 10 years, I was a vocal community activist with the Downtown Eastside Residents' Association. These were not hypothetical policy debates. They were immediate and urgent. We were working on life and death issues. Government decisions directly impact real people. Lives hung in the balance. We were highly political, just not yet at the decision-making table.

I didn't even know that was politics. I thought it was just fighting for something you believed in.

CAROLYN BENNETT

Before being elected as an MP in 1997 for the Liberal Party, Carolyn Bennett was a family physician in Toronto, an assistant professor at the University of Toronto, and a board member of Women's College Hospital, the Ontario Medical Association, and the Medico-Legal Society of Toronto.

I had never, ever thought of being in politics. It wasn't something my family did or knew. It happened after my fight to save Women's College Hospital. The Liberals asked me to run. When I replied I knew nothing about politics, they retorted, "What do you think you just did for Women's College?" I didn't even know that was politics. I thought it was just fighting for something you believed in.

I decided this was the time to convert my academic theory and community activism into policy.

SHUBHA SANDILL

Prior to seeking the nomination for the Liberal Party in the 2019 federal election, Shubha Sandill was heavily involved with community and political activism in Hamilton and has fundraised for the Liberal Party.

Five years ago, when I was completing my gender and public policy research at York University, I first stumbled on the topic of women's political participation. I had no idea where this would lead me. Within the same month, my daughter, an executive on the Ontario Bar Association's Women Lawyers Forum, invited me to their event "Pathways to Power: Women in Politics" with panellists such as Barbara Hall [former mayor of Toronto] and Martha Hall Findlay [former Liberal MP]. After a coffee meeting with Findlay, I gained practical insights into what it was like for women in politics. When two long-term party members approached me to run for federal politics, I decided this was the time to convert my academic theory and community activism into policy. There were tough lessons ahead, but I was ready.

SHERI BENSON

Sheri Benson, former CEO of the United Way in Saskatoon, was elected as an MP in 2015 for the NDP. She was the first openly queer candidate in Saskatchewan to be elected to the House of Commons.

You're such a nice person. Why would you want to run for politics?

W omen who work in non-profit organizations, and a large number of women relative to men do, have a particular path they need to learn to navigate between the world of non-partisan charity work and the life of a partisan politician. If you cherish networks and friendships, the nature of both may change. Some people even offered an opinion: "Sheri, you're such a nice person. Why would you want to run for politics?" You become aware of ideological divisions, which you were accustomed to rising above.

There are other obvious barriers. NGO boards are dependent on grants and donations. They need to walk a careful non-partisan line. Not many, in my experience, have developed policies to give guidance to employees on how to take leave and transition into politics.

There is a financial side to this transition too. Entering politics is regarded with some caution money-wise. Women working in the charitable sector and non-profits usually do not earn a great deal of money. Entering politics carries a financial burden, especially if a leave without pay is required during nominations and campaigns.

Yet women working in non-profit agencies have extraordinary insight into communities and can bring excellent value to the table. They may not be doctors or lawyers or MBAs, but they know their issues and carry an important voice. These women need support for a good transition if we intend to maximize Canada's potential to reach parity in politics. Non-profit sector agencies have values that promote equity and fight for human rights. The very essence of many community organizations is about fighting discrimination. So, in this regard, the fit is natural.

I found the path often lonely. But I was deeply humbled and honoured when citizens elected me their MP. Public office is an extraordinary privilege.

> ## My journey began before I was born.

ROSEANNE ARCHIBALD

In 2018, RoseAnne Archibald of Taykwa Tagamou Nation was elected Ontario Regional Chief at the 44th annual All Ontario Chiefs conference in Nipissing First Nation, representing 133 First Nations communities across the province. Archibald was formerly Chief for Taykwa Tagamou Nation, Deputy Grand Chief of the Nishnawbe-Aski Nation, and Grand Chief for Mushkegowuk Council.

My journey began before I was born. My grandfather was Chief in the days when leadership was hereditary. My father became the first democratically elected Chief in our community. Service and leadership were deeply ingrained in our family.

I became politically active as a student involved in the national hunger strike protesting federal changes to First Nations post-secondary education. A secondary outcome of my activism was being viewed as a fierce advocate and leader early on. In 1990, I was elected Chief and became both the first woman and the youngest Chief at 23 years. But I was not ready. I stepped down.

Five months later, I was approached to run for Deputy Grand Chief for Nishnawbe-Aski Nation and three years later Grand Chief for Mushkegowuk Council. Each step deepened my leadership skills, and at each stage I was inspired by strong women, including my mother. I was fortunate to be mentored by evolved and progressive men who embraced women's leadership.

My commitment to cultivating women's leadership was advanced as member of the Assembly of First Nations (AFN) Women's Council. Three AFN Women's Summits have since convened. As the current Regional Chief of Ontario, parity in portfolio and Chiefs committees is a goal. I also look forward to building on the Women's Development Project launched in 2006 by Nishnawbe Aski Nation (NAN) with Ontario Trillium Foundation focused on Personal Capacity Building and Leadership Development for First Nations Women.

Of the 133 Chiefs in Ontario, about one-third are now women. I'm grateful that male leaders have helped make space for women, in this colonial system, and strong women have stepped forward to lead. It is important not only to open that space, but to hold that space for other women leaders. Projects like NAN Women's Development Project and the past and present work of Equaywuk seek not only to open the door — but to take the hinges off the door so that women, if they choose, can freely walk into the halls of power.

KAREN MCCRIMMON

Karen McCrimmon was the first woman air navigator and first to command a Canadian Forces flying squadron. McCrimmon retired from the Canadian Forces in 2006 and was elected as an MP for Kanata-Carleton in 2015 for the Liberal Party.

My point of entry into politics is solidly planted in my military service to the nation.

My point of entry into politics is solidly planted in my military service to the nation. If I compare my professional career in the military with life in politics, I can draw many crossover skills. Both involve discipline and calculated risk. The more discipline you bring to campaigns and time management in executing your mandate as an MP, the better the odds are that you will achieve your goals.

While the consequences are vastly different between military deployment and politics, they both involve a measure of calculated risk. You can't control all the moving parts all at once. Some things are out of your control. The goal is to bring excellence to the pieces that you do control. A military background gives you this platform.

LISA RAITT

Before being elected as a Conservative MP in 2008, Lisa Raitt was the president and CEO of the Toronto Port Authority (TPA), now PortsToronto. Raitt was named Deputy Leader of the Official Opposition in 2017.

It is important to bring skills from the corporate world into politics. For sure, this is not an easy decision to take. The touted claim that being in politics will enhance and advance your private sector career is not necessarily the case. Entering politics may significantly curtail opportunities for re-entry on the corporate track you were cultivating. For some, the remuneration will never match a highly successful career in business.

But the rewards in politics are immeasurable. Women bring significant skills to politics as mediators, team players, and consensus builders. Coming from business we also add skills in navigating the regulatory world. Issues of critical importance to women like childcare and eldercare, housing, poverty, and pay equity are, at their heart, economic issues. They all should be a part of the business agenda of a nation.

"It is important to bring skills from the corporate world into politics.

Politics and Identity

For many women, mounting political campaigns means more than just managing sexism and systemic barriers due to their gender. Women may also face political hardships and discrimination because of factors that include their race, ethnicity, class, ability, sexuality, and faith. Intersectionality — a term coined by Kimberlé Crenshaw in 1989, after decades of scholarship by Black, Indigenous, and feminists of colour — refers to this broader reality. A professor of law at UCLA and Columbia Law School and a leading authority on civil rights, Crenshaw originally used the word to help explain, in a legal setting, the oppression that African American women face. In her 2016 TED talk, 27 years later, she spoke to the urgency of understanding intersectionality, that those who "[stand] in the path of multiple forms of exclusion [are] likely to get hit by both."

While multiculturalism defines the character of our nation, moving past tolerance and ensuring inclusion requires an understanding of intersectionality. In 1995, I was one of the thousands of participants at the Beijing Fourth World Conference on Women who crafted a global policy framework, the Beijing Platform for Action, to help guide and commit nations to gender equality.

ANJU DHILLON

Anju Dhillon is the first Sikh Canadian to practise law in Quebec courts and the first South Asian woman to be elected to any of the three levels of government in Quebec. Dhillon won a seat in 2015 for Dorval-Lachine-LaSalle for the federal Liberal Party.

When I was growing up, my family (when I say family, I include parents and grandparents because they also had a hand in my upbringing) always taught me to be respectful of others — to treat everyone equally because we are all in the image of God; to work hard and help those in need; to always stay in high spirits no matter how bad a situation may get. My father always said, "You can do anything a boy can." This was my upbringing. Only when I started attending school and went through the experiences I did, I learned I was different from others. My family had immigrated to Canada from Punjab, India, in the 1970s. I was the first Sikh lawyer to practise law in the courts of Quebec.

On October 19, 2015, I became not only the first Sikh but also the first South Asian to ever be elected out of the federal and provincial levels of government in the history of Quebec. It had always been my dream to become a member of Parliament. At the time I ran, the thought was always with me that there was so much at stake, not only about winning my own seat — although that was a big part of it — but what my winning would mean to the youth of the South Asian community and other visible minority communities. For me, I considered it a hurdle that had not yet been overcome by those residing in Quebec. I would think to myself, "If you succeed, you could open the door for other South Asians and ethnic minorities." If they saw I could do it, they could also have hope that they had a chance to participate in public life. In the same way, my becoming a lawyer motivated others who were unsure of pursuing that path. My being elected an MP would also give them the courage to take up the challenge to run in politics and one day succeed.

> ## If they saw I could do it, they could also have hope that they had a chance to participate in public life.

It is my fervent hope that other people, especially women with a similar background, now know anything is possible. Women already have many challenges to overcome just based on their gender, but when there is intersectionality, such as someone being a visible minority, in the LGBTQ2+ community, or handicapped, the lack of possibilities becomes much more significant, and the challenges become a deterrent. Not everyone may be as fortunate as I was, where my parents made many sacrifices for me and always encouraged me and believed in my dreams.

FARHEEN KHAN

In 2015, Farheen Khan took the federal NDP nomination in the riding of Mississauga Centre in Ontario. After the election, Khan founded "Muslims Actually," a campaign and blog (now incorporated into Muslim Link) "to share positive images of Muslims and their stories through social media."

After 9/11, I was attacked. It was not an easy time. Making the decision to enter politics in 2015 put my image and physical security under additional scrutiny and threat. I was a woman and a Muslim who chose to wear a hijab. I lacked a safety net of strong family support or broad personal networks and was working on violence against women. When it came down to the bottom line, I wanted to do something significant. Taking a stand and running politically was that line.

Media followed me to doors. I was challenging stereotypes. On my documents, I listed my credentials, mentioning my sister was in the army and my father was in the police. On my brochure, my picture was placed between leaders Tom Mulcair and Jack Layton. Still, we had to find non-racialized canvassers to open the door. Then, I could do my part. But we had to navigate that hurdle.

If you are committed to an anti-racist feminist framework, it is your responsibility to bring marginalized people into the centre of the conversation. When supporting women, everyone else marginalized gets supported by extension: women of colour, women victims of violence, women living in poverty. Together, these lenses all contribute to making sounder judgments.

" It is your responsibility to bring marginalized people into the centre of the conversation.

KATHLEEN WYNNE

Kathleen Wynne was elected as a school board trustee in 2000 and elected as an MPP for the Ontario Liberal Party for Don Valley West in 2003. She held various cabinet positions before becoming premier in 2013. Wynne was the first woman to be premier of Ontario and Canada's first openly gay premier.

I n my leadership bid, I wanted people to know I was a lesbian. I wanted to express my confidence in the openness of people in this province. I trust that people, if given the chance, will rise. If I lose any election, I don't believe it will be because I am gay. We are an open and accepting society, and it is our job as legislators to live up to that vision — and, by example, call others to the same standards.

If you deny the truth, that's exactly how homophobia works. It works because people get afraid and step back. I believe there are more people who want to be inclusive than those who do not. After becoming premier, wherever I went, people would come up to me and say I had given their son or daughter courage to be who they are. That has meant the world to me.

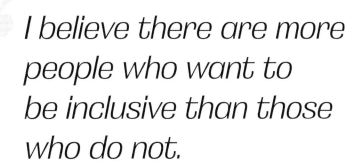

I believe there are more people who want to be inclusive than those who do not.

CELINA CAESAR-CHAVANNES

Taking care of personal mental and physical health in any line of work, including politics, is essential. Celina Caesar-Chavannes, MP from 2015 to 2019 (Liberal 2015 to 2019, Independent 2019), shared her experience with depression in the *Huffington Post*.

Mental health is as real as a broken bone. It needs to be destigmatized and managed with knowledge and compassion. Luckily, I had both present in my personal and professional life. In the middle of all the headlines and hard work, I suffer and struggle with a depressive disorder. After the by-election defeat in 2014 and during my first mandate as a member in Parliament, I had a major crisis. I wrote about it on my blog. Many citizens responded with gratefulness that I had made public what they had been struggling with silently. I was not sure I could climb out of the dark hole I was in. I was so lucky to have my husband who stepped in with the children and family finances to provide stability and support. The prime minister, who understands mental health first-hand through his courageous mother, was incredibly supportive. It is important to speak forthrightly and support those of us dealing with mental health. It is just as real and important as physical health.

> *It is important to speak forthrightly and support those of us dealing with mental health. It is just as real and important as physical health.*

RANA BOKHARI

When Rana Bokhari was elected leader of the Manitoba Liberal Party in 2013, she became the first woman of colour to lead a provincial political party in Canada. After stepping down, Bokhari gave a TEDx talk, "Leadership: Breaking Traditional Gender, Age, and Religious Barriers," to shed light on the racism and sexism that she experienced while in politics.

When girls see women leaders who look like them on the path ahead, it helps prepare the way. Nobody looked like me. At the time I ran for party leadership, there were no young women of colour anywhere in a leadership role. Definitely not in Manitoba.

> *When girls see women leaders who look like them on the path ahead, it helps prepare the way.*

I asked myself, "Why is this? Why are women of colour not doing this?" It's not a competency issue. Regardless of age, race, or culture, the talent is there. The real question is, why aren't there more women, and women of colour in electoral politics? It took until 2013 for the first female minority leader in Canadian history to be a woman of colour, and that was me. At a minimum, I provided a visible change at the top of party leadership. Now the question is, how did that change things? How can we speed up the future entry of women, and especially women of colour, into politics? What are we doing? As one step on that path, we are visible models for others to see ahead of them. We are helping prepare the way.

I seized the opportunity to use the space that I occupied as leader of the party while I held the position. Political power is temporary. It is important to use power purposefully.

> "I am a worker, a woman, and Black. ... And when I speak, I will be informed by all that I am.

MARLENE JENNINGS

Elected in 1997, Marlene Jennings is the first Black woman from Quebec to be elected to the House of Commons. Jennings served five terms as MP for Notre-Dame-de-Grâce-Lachine, Quebec, from 1997 to 2011 for the Liberal Party.

I never disclaimed being a woman or being Black. That is who I am. It informs my point of view just as does being a former unionized worker. When asked, "Are you going to be working on Black issues?" I would reply, "I am multidimensional. I am a worker, a woman, and Black. I am also a lawyer and a mother and a community activist. I will speak on all issues — economic, health, transport, aging — all issues. And when I speak, I will be informed by all that I am." I do not ever disclaim or discount who I am.

I served five terms in Parliament and always remained exactly and completely who I was. To disclaim being a woman? It is precisely because of the feminists before me that women won the right to the vote, and I could be a member of Parliament. Why would I ever silence the history that made it possible for me to run for elected office? Think before you speak. Think twice if you are emotional about that issue. And never disclaim who you are!

Just like when people asked, "How can you be a mother and also a member of Parliament?" I responded by being exactly who I am: "Yes, I am a mother. My own mother, who never had a chance to obtain her high school education, was the smartest woman I ever knew, bar none! My entire extended family supported me and my daughter — the family pitched in to make it all happen. Was it challenging? Of course. Was it worth it? It was a priceless life honour."

JEAN YIP

Jean Yip was elected as an MP for the Liberal Party in a by-election for the Scarborough-Agincourt riding in December 2017, a seat previously held by her late husband, who died in office.

Born in Scarborough, I am proud to represent Scarborough-Agincourt. I am one of the first Chinese Canadian women MPs born in Canada. I am aware of the importance of augmenting the presence of visible minority members and their issues in Ottawa. It is my privilege to bring this voice and my life experience to Parliament. I never felt I was campaigning differently because I was a woman or a visible minority — it was just me running with a great team. It is important to reflect the diversity in my riding. I am still awed by the amount of support and confidence for me. Most of all, I am so thankful to the people of Scarborough-Agincourt who have placed their trust in me.

It is important to reflect the diversity in my riding.

Never Doubt Yourself

Even with a list of impressive credentials, a history of community service, and an abundance of formative life experiences, the women interviewed for this book, when invited to run, often asked, "Isn't there someone else more qualified?" Positions of power have historically excluded women. Women's voices and achievements have largely gone unacknowledged in history textbooks. When you're an outlier, self-doubt gives rise to hesitation. Presenting yourself as a political candidate might seem presumptuous, as if you were imposing on a space reserved for others. Dubbed the "imposter syndrome," the solution is to populate spaces with women — and with women of diverse backgrounds. The rise of #MeToo and the return of "The Year of the Woman" in American politics are inspiring women to overcome their doubts and enter the political ring. Organizations across Canada, including Equal Voice, are equipping and empowering women to enable this rising tide of women putting their name on the ballot.

I was sure there were more qualified people than me, and immediately I began suggesting names.

KELLY REGAN

Prior to being elected as an MLA for the Nova Scotia Liberal Party in 2009, Kelly Regan worked as a television director, producer, and writer. When she was asked to run politically, she quickly recommended others who might be better candidates.

When our leader, Stephen McNeil, approached me and asked if I would run provincially, I initially said no. I was sure there were more qualified people than me, and immediately I began suggesting names.

After I said no, I initially felt relief, and then … not. A couple of days later, I went to the church. The minister (whom I had consulted in my decision-making process) spoke about the "Parable of the Talents" from St. Matthew. I realized I needed to remember that as an elected member, I would be there to look after the resources — both human and monetary — of Nova Scotia. I knew that if I could remember that, I would be a good member. I knew in that moment that I could do this job.

I knew there would be real challenges for a family with three children and a husband already in politics, who was often away from home. We made the decision as a family. Then I talked to the person recruiting for the party and let her know: "I'm in. Let's do this."

ANNE MCLELLAN

Dalhousie University chancellor, University of Alberta law professor, and Deputy Prime Minister for the Liberal Party are among Anne McLellan's accomplishments. McLellan served four terms as a an MP for Edmonton Northwest, Edmonton West, and Edmonton Centre from 1993 to 2006.

You might look around and ask, "Should I be here?"

There's no question, historically, in rooms filled with mainly men in politics, you might look around and ask, "Should I be here? Why am I here?" Hopefully women of this generation ask this question less. They've been brought up in a different environment.

I was raised in a small rural community in Nova Scotia. Everyone knew the McLellans were Liberal. At the turn of the last century, we were known as Laurier Liberals. My mom was deputy reeve of the county. Our family was always surrounded by politics. I was always involved with the party, just not as a candidate.

After I moved to Alberta and was practising law, one day a woman showed up in my office. She had heard me speak about the Canadian Charter of Rights and Freedoms. She said, "I think you should think about the federal nomination in the next election." Of course, I gave that no thought because the Liberals hadn't been elected in Alberta for 25 years. "Why would I hit my head against that wall?" I thought to myself. But I eventually did, survived a nomination, and went on to win the riding by 11 votes.

NICOLE SARAUER

In 2017, when the provincial leader of the Saskatchewan NDP stepped down, Nicole Sarauer was appointed the interim leader of the party and held the role until Ryan Meili was elected leader in 2018. Sarauer was the first woman to lead the party in Saskatchewan.

When the moment came to dive into a leadership race and, if successful, lead my party in a provincial election, I paused. Should I go back to school and become better qualified to lead? I chose to ignore this impulse, then found myself as party leader, counselling others to face down the same demons.

I kept Dr. Valerie Young's book *The Secret Thoughts of Successful Women: Why Capable People Suffer from the Imposter Syndrome and How to Thrive in Spite of It* close at hand. It examines how doubt curtails women's performance and maps strategies to reclaim top performance.

> *The political space seems reserved for others. Stepping into that space seems like intruding.*

It was my responsibility to erase the echo chamber in caucus and committees through active listening and recognition of all ideas. The next piece was to ignore the debilitating experience of feeling like an imposter. Women have not historically seen themselves reflected at the decision-making tables of politics. The political space seems reserved for others. Stepping into that space seems like intruding. Breaking this feeling is easier said than done. Overcoming the imposter syndrome involves breaking through bastions of traditional power.

AUDREY MCLAUGHLIN

The first woman in Canada to be elected head of a federal political party, Audrey McLaughlin worked to recruit a diverse roster of candidates to the NDP. The gendered difference between men and women in response to her outreach struck her.

T he "dragon of doubt" is planted even at an early age. I, too, find myself a victim of its suggestive power.

As leader of the federal NDP Party, I encouraged a vigorous search for talented candidates across the country. I placed a special focus on finding community-based women leaders to ask them to consider federal politics. I generalize, but I was struck by the contrast in responses. Men wondered how they would handle the power. Women asked how they would manage the responsibility. They doubted themselves from the outset and were quick to offer names of others before themselves. Overcoming doubt seemed to be our starting point.

Speaking at public schools about women's leadership, it is doubly worrisome for me to see how the messaging coming at girls and promoted in magazines, in ads, online, and on billboards repeats all the ways girls can become more attractive and accepted. In its worst form, online shaming and bullying have had tragic outcomes.

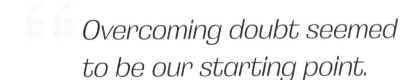

Overcoming doubt seemed to be our starting point.

Run, Ask, or Support

Many women in this book have attested to how the support of others was critical in their decision to seek nomination for political office. My mother, Eileen "Stevie" McGregor, spent her whole life asking and supporting other women to enter politics. Inspiring other women to run, equipping them, and empowering them to succeed can help close the gender gap.

The UN's "Division for the Advancement of Women" says that "women are also less likely to present themselves as candidates, often seeing themselves as lacking the skills necessary to perform well in politics." But research continues to show that when women are on the ballot, they win at the same rate as men. The challenge is at the start — getting women on the ballot.

Each one of us can make a difference in political life in Canada by inviting one of the extraordinary women who surround us to step up and run — and to support them when they do.

Why wouldn't you like to be on the inside making a difference rather than standing on the outside knocking on the door?

HEDY FRY

Hedy Fry practised family medicine in Vancouver for more than 20 years. As the MP for Vancouver Centre for the Liberal Party, Fry was first elected in 1993 and is the longest-serving woman MP in Canadian history.

I was in medicine. I never wanted to do politics. Serendipitously, Jean Chrétien asked me if I would run. I said no. Twice more he asked me. Twice more, I said no. The third time, he said, "You're an activist and always pushing the envelope. Why wouldn't you like to be on the inside making a difference rather than standing on the outside knocking on the door?" I asked him, "Can I do that?" He said, "Yes." So, I asked him, if I ran, would he amend the Canadian Human Rights Act and add sexual orientation as prohibited grounds for discrimination? I had seen the suffering and inequity the LGBTQ2 + community faced. I went through the 1980s AIDS epidemic with my patients. I knew we had to change things. I asked him to guarantee it. The rest is history.

SHERI BENSON

Sheri Benson was CEO of the local United Way when she was first asked if she had ever considered running for politics. In 2015, Benson became an MP for the NDP in Saskatoon West.

At every opportunity I have, I invite women to consider elected positions in their future.

A colleague decided to run for our Federation of Labour president. She turned to me and said, "Why don't you run?" I thought she was crazy, and of course, I didn't run. But I had a couple of moments when people reflected back to me that I might have leadership abilities. It gave me pause to think. I never thought of myself that way. I enjoyed working in the community. I loved having different folks around the table. I worked my whole career in a non-partisan environment.

If you told me in June of 2014 that I would be running for office, I would not have believed you. I was the CEO for United Way. But I had a very insightful board member ask me, "What's next for you, Sheri?" We had been really struggling to get our homelessness plan moving in Saskatchewan and really trying to get governments to understand and come to the table for what we felt was an awesome leadership opportunity for community and business and government to work together. But things were not happening.

So, when that board member said, "What's next?" I thought, what is next after the United Way? I wondered where I might have impact. A second conversation happened around that time. My MLA reached out to me for coffee and asked if I had ever thought about running. Those two conversations started me thinking. I started to have conversations with other people asking if they could see me having an impact in elected office. I reached out to people who I knew would give me a really honest answer. I asked each one "Does this look like something that I could do?" They were all positive. I would be 55 in January. I thought, If I'm going to really make a big change, I'm going to have to do it now. It just seemed like the right time, and I might really regret if I didn't try.

So, I decided to take it one step at a time and run for nomination without looking too far down the track. And here I am. I know I have a very privileged position as a member of Parliament, so at every opportunity I have, I invite women to consider elected positions in their future. I trust that I'm going to use this privilege in a way that I hope is helpful to as many others as I can while I have the chance.

CANDICE BERGEN

First elected to the House of Commons in 2008, Candice Bergen was re-elected in 2011 and 2015 for the Conservative Party, representing the riding of Portage-Lisgar, Manitoba. In 2016, Bergen was appointed House Leader for the Official Opposition.

I've met so many impressive women. Each time I ask them if they have ever considered running.

A few months after I joined the party, I got a call from a woman named Joyce Chilton, the president of the riding association. There was only a very small Canadian Alliance association. She left me a message: "We have never met. I see you joined the party, and you are part of our area. We're having our Annual General Meeting (AGM), and we'd love to have you. We need to get more women involved in politics."

That's when I heard the little voice inside my head, my mom's voice, saying, "Candice, you joined. You need to go even if you don't want to be involved. At least go to the AGM." My husband and I were going to dinner that night. I said to him, "Why don't you drop me off at the AGM? I'll be there for half an hour, and then we'll go for dinner." Half an hour later, when he picked me up, I was on the board. I think I was the secretary. That was the start of it, and that was in 2000. I've met so many impressive women. Each time I ask them if they have ever considered running. I advise other women in leadership and men in leadership to ask women if they had considered running because most women will not have given it thought. It takes a number of asks for us to really think about it seriously.

KEMI AKAPO

In 2018, Kemi Akapo was elected as a city councillor in Peterborough, the first Black woman to be elected to Peterborough's city council. Before entering municipal politics, Akapo sat on the board of the YWCA Peterborough Haliburton and was the Settlement Services Coordinator at Peterborough's New Canadians Centre.

I f she can see it, she will believe it. For so many, seeing is believing. Belief is powerful. As a young girl growing up and seeing my mother exhibit strength and courage in various situations, it made me believe that one day I, too, could do the same. In fact, I never doubted the fact that I could. I just always thought it was so because I saw it modelled in my life. It was this belief, in part, which led me to run for city council in Peterborough in 2018.

As I got more involved in community organizations in Peterborough and learned more about the role of city council, I realized how intertwined everything is and how city council's decisions have broad impact. Having been on boards and worked in various organizations, I knew the importance of having diverse views represented. People began suggesting to me that I should run. They felt I could bring a voice that was not well represented on council. Having seen other young women run before me and succeed, it boosted me to think that I could run too. It made me think, as a Black woman, how seeing me run for politics could inspire other Black women and women of colour to run. Perhaps I could be their inspiration as my mother was to me.

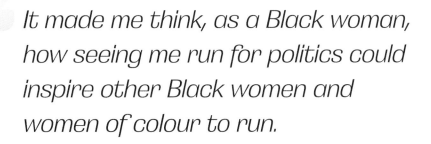

It made me think, as a Black woman, how seeing me run for politics could inspire other Black women and women of colour to run.

ANDREA HORWATH

Andrea Horwath was a community organizer — working closely with the Hamilton labour movement providing English as an Additional Language (EAL) training for workers — before becoming a three-time Hamilton city councillor and MPP in 2004 for the Ontario NDP. She went on to win provincial party leadership in 2009.

Succeeding in reaching a caucus of 50 percent women in the 2018 election roster did not happen by accident. The NDP built a process that required every riding to undertake a vigorous candidate search with special attention to gender and diversity. In fact, local riding associations had to show documentation of this extensive outreach and interview process before a nomination meeting was called.

We required an accountability. It wasn't something we wished to see. It was something we required to see. That's why we have great women like Catherine Fife, Cheri DiNovo, and Peggy Sattler. It's hard work to attract talented women into politics. Women do not automatically see themselves in this arena. Their first response is often "Why me?" I have found that men are much more easily persuaded. Many assume the space is open for them and wonder why I hadn't asked them sooner. Women need more persuasion.

It is our responsibility to seek out diverse and inclusive slates of candidates and achieve gender parity in our slates and in winnable ridings. Our commitment to equity has always been more than just numbers.

> *It's hard work to attract talented women into politics. Women do not automatically see themselves in this arena.*

DEB GREY

After initially rebuffing the idea of running for office, in 1989, Deb Grey went on to become the Reform Party's first MP. Grey served as an MP for more than 15 years and became, in 2000, the first-ever woman to be Leader of the Official Opposition.

I was a new teacher at a school just south of the river. My friend Liz called and said, "Deb, we have a new riding and no candidate. Why don't you run?" I replied, "Liz, that's ridiculous. First, I'm a teacher, and it's September. I love teaching, make sufficient money, and have good holidays. Why would I heap abuse on myself by becoming a politician?" Liz came right back at me, saying, "We don't have a candidate, and I think you'd do a great job." I thanked her for her vote of confidence, then went home and did my lesson plan for Grade 12 English.

But Liz was persistent. She got onto the phone to Pat Chern, who lived over in Smoky Lake and was president of the riding association. I didn't even know what a riding association was. She handed the phone to me. "Hello," Pat said. "It's great you are thinking of becoming a candidate." I quickly replied that I'd be interested in maybe voting for Reform, if I agreed with the principles and policies and if she sent me a copy of the platform.

Surely there can be no more unpredictable path than this story of how I arrived in Parliament. There I was, barely back in school by a couple of days. The federal member, John Dahmer, unfortunately died. A by-election was needed. I said, "No, I'm not doing a by-election. First of all, my school board will likely fire me. Secondly, Preston Manning lives close by. He should run. I'll help him."

It was the first of December. The weather in northern Alberta was getting ugly. Despite this, Preston Manning drove all over this big, sprawling rural riding talking to people in gas stations and stores. He explained we were heading into a by-election and wondered what they thought about Deborah Grey. People told Preston they'd be willing to take a shot on me. He came back to me saying, "Deborah, I think it would be good if you would run." I was stunned. He persisted. He kept asking. I was just learning as I went along. But Mr. Manning knew everything about the party. He had great confidence in me, researched people's reaction to me, and then asked again if I would run. That's how it all began. He kept asking until my firm "No" became an eventual "Yes!" Then my unlikely journey in politics began.

NANCY PECKFORD

In 2018, Nancy Peckford was elected the first woman mayor of the amalgamated municipality of North Grenville. Peckford is the national spokesperson and executive director of Equal Voice, an organization dedicated to electing more women at all levels of political office in Canada.

A part of the goals of Equal Voice, in its mission to elect more women ... is to celebrate those men who are partners in achieving this vision.

A part of the goals of Equal Voice, in its mission to elect more women across the nation to Parliament, is to celebrate those men who are partners in achieving this vision. NDP Leader Jack Layton was an exceptional champion of women in politics in Canada. He dedicated significant energy recruiting women to run, and he matched his commitment with actions. An Equal Voice letter posted to the website at the time of his death paid tribute to this leadership.

During his leadership, women were appointed to senior party and caucus positions, including Judy Wasylycia-Leis as Canada's first female federal finance critic, followed by MP Peggy Nash. MP Libby Davies was appointed by Mr. Layton as House Leader and Deputy Leader. In party structure, his chief of staff and director of strategic communications were women. Mr. Layton also recommended that newly elected MP Nycole Turmel serve as interim leader of the Official Opposition in 2011, the second woman to hold this position. Upon his death, she became Leader of the Official Opposition until the election of NDP leader Thomas Mulcair in 2012. In 2011, Equal Voice recognized Jack Layton as one of three champions celebrated on the occasion of its tenth anniversary.

Part 2

WHAT DOES IT TAKE?

*D*istractions abound in political races. Contestants enter the race, then drop out. Energy levels peak, then subside. Party popularity climbs, then falls. Competitors change their tactics. Leaders' debates are broadcast, headlines come and go, and poll numbers change again. There is the constant temptation to focus elsewhere and plenty of opportunity to do so. It takes your mind off the task at hand.

I grew up on Clear Lake in the Kawartha Lakes region of Ontario, competing in Sunday afternoon sailing races. I had a yellow sail. Facing turbulent waters and unexpected events on the race course was just a part of it all. Early on, I learned the cost of getting distracted. The yellow sail is an image to help campaigns bypass distractions, stay on course, and keep the focus on their own "sail" — their campaign values and goals.

After you decide to run, understanding how the political process works is essential to planning a winning campaign strategy. This section is designed to help you get started. It introduces innovative training opportunities open to women, explores the range of networks that women can mobilize, speaks to the nomination process, provides advice on campaigning, and tells door-to-door canvassing stories. This section concludes with a glimpse into the world of leadership races: what it takes to survive, and sometimes win, at the top. In the Appendix (page 218), you will find a practical roadmap for potential candidates. It was developed by Harry Mortimer, an accountant who provides advisory services related to the Canada Elections Act. He outlines the steps to take throughout the pre-election period, the election campaign, and post-election.

Images from the Daughters
of the Vote Program, hosted
by Equal Voice Canada —
International Women's Day,
8 March 2017

Training, Networks, and Mentors

The ability to build teams, communicate clearly, and arrive at consensus across diverse communities are all valuable skills, but these skills alone will not win elections. Undergoing training, including training on election rules, fundraising, managing volunteers, the media, canvassing, and debating, is essential to a successful election campaign. Political campaigns in Canada at all levels are governed by election laws and policies, the most important being the Canada Elections Act; breaking these rules could result in criminal charges (and your seat).

A wide variety of creative campaign training workshops tailored to women are available across Canada and internationally for all levels of government. Political parties, non-governmental organizations (NGOs), and university campuses offer practical resources and networking opportunities for women as they assess the route and get ready for the journey. A list is provided in the Appendix (page 224).

But campaign training is not the only thing that is necessary; networks and mentors are fundamental to the success of a political campaign. Networks can range from sporting and hobby groups to alumni and business organizations. Their work can include selling memberships for a nomination, raising money for a campaign, and building teams to pull the vote; women entering politics need these supportive networks. Candidates and campaigns will benefit from a strong base of contacts, personal and professional, online and in person. Tapping into them, building them, and leveraging them are important campaign skills.

Several of the women I interviewed mentioned building a network of community advisers at the outset of their entry into politics. Before filling out the papers to run, many women reached out to convene a "kitchen cabinet" of advisers by drawing on a broad cross-section of community leaders. However, men's networks tend to be more robust and well resourced; as well, fewer women have run and been elected at the local, provincial, and national levels. Political parties have sought to bridge this gap by encouraging local associations to open riding groups, establishing women's commissions nationally, and creating a women's caucus at the party level.

> **"**
> *Networking is a skill that women entering politics need to build.*

KARA LEVIS

Kara Levis was the 2019 Alberta Party candidate for Calgary-Klein in the provincial election. She was president of the National Liberal Women's Commission (2016–2018) and a former board member of the Association of Women Lawyers and the Ask Her Association.

Networking is a skill that women entering politics need to build. There are different kinds of networks helpful to any campaign. It's important for women to cultivate connections to business networks and community organizations. These networks are resources for understanding issues in the community as well as possible donors. Another type of network is the circles of friends and colleagues who often become central to building a campaign team. These networks involve the candidate much more directly. A third set of networks involves building relationships inside the party structure. These networks can give a candidate the most direct channel to knowledge and information about the party and campaign resources. All three types of networks are helpful tools.

We also need more women inside the party structure running for positions. I always have this advice for women: "Just go out and do it. Find a party or a candidate or a political movement that speaks to you. You could fall anywhere on the political spectrum. Go out and start volunteering. Start getting involved. Volunteering your time will be welcomed. Join a party, help out, then run for a position."

When I joined the Liberal riding association in Calgary in 2012, it was a small core group of dedicated volunteers. I dove into policy and became the policy director on the local board. Two years later, I went to the 2014 National Policy Convention in Montreal. In

Alberta, I then co-chaired the party convention and attended the AGM of the Alberta Women's Commission happening at the Convention. I put my name forward to be president and was acclaimed.

CAROL HUGHES

Carol Hughes has represented the riding of Algoma-Manitoulin-Kapuskasing in Ontario in the House of Commons since 2008. Prior to being elected, Hughes was a regional representative for the Canadian Labour Congress (CLC) and ran as the NDP candidate in the 2004 election and the 2006 election.

It's important to reach out to women early in their thinking to offer campaign training and teach campaign skills.

I was a staff member with the Canadian Labour Congress during my career and am very aware and proud of the work the CLC does in designing educational programs for individuals, especially women, who are considering entering politics in Canada. It is very helpful to have this type of specific outreach to women in unions and communities to encourage their involvement at all levels of government. It's important to reach out to women early in their thinking to offer campaign training and teach campaign skills. The CLC plays an important role for women in Canada.

My work with the CLC included specific training on how to run certain campaigns focused on women's issues or advocating for better working conditions for women and addressing some of the inequities that women face.

There are other workers' unions, as well, that give specific courses to encourage women to get involved in politics. That is something that many of the unions do. They will approach locals or union members asking a question like "Is there anybody in your local that you would recommend who is quite active and that we could court to become members?" Unions look for people who have some type of recognition within the community. The NDP is very good at seeking and recruiting women to run for political office. More importantly, they recruit women for key ridings — winnable ridings. It's not about just having a woman run to add to their numbers. I was impacted by this clear commitment both in recruitment and in party platform.

We all collaborate, across party lines, to engage women in electoral politics.

CATHERINE FIFE

Catherine Fife was elected as an MPP for the Ontario NDP for Kitchener-Waterloo in 2012, followed by two more terms for Waterloo. Fife has been involved in the Waterloo Region Women's Municipal Campaign School "learnhowtorun.com" for women considering running for public office.

In our area, campaign training is hosted at city hall for all women interested in learning about running for municipal, provincial, or federal politics. We all collaborate, across party lines, to engage women in electoral politics. Many of us received a great deal of advice and encouragement through these workshops. We are now giving back our experience to the event as mentors with the goal to attract and train more women. Our vision is to open the door for young women for the future.

Go out into your community and serve. Be engaged in local organizations first — then come to politics.

JENNIFER POLLOCK

Called to the Alberta Bar in 2004, Jennifer Pollock opened a private practice the following year. Pollock was a federal candidate for the Liberal Party in Calgary West in 2006 and 2008 and in Calgary Centre in 2011.

In Calgary, "Winning Women" [a group of Calgary organizations, including the YWCA and the Calgary Board of Education] used to host a conference once a year. Participants had the opportunity to network and meet women politicians. Each participant was given a *Winning Women Handbook* on how to run for election. There were sections for school board, municipal, provincial, and federal races. Sessions included how to budget for campaigns. The speakers shared practical advice. One inspiring panellist [in 1991] was Alexa McDonough. When she finished speaking, someone from the audience posed a question. After listing all the political science courses he had taken and all the campaigns he had worked on, he asked for advice on what to do next to run for office.

I never forgot Alexa McDonough's answer: "Get a life." By this she meant "Go out into your community and serve. Be engaged in local organizations first — then come to politics." Some humorous advice surfaced too. Someone offered, "Don't change your hairstyle during the campaign. Keep them focused on your policy." It was serious advice. Women tend to get critiqued on what we wear and how we look. Keep them focused on your principles and the content of your policies. What counts is not your clothes; it's your character.

ANITA VANDENBELD

Anita Vandenbeld worked at equipping and training women for politics around the world. She was elected to Parliament in 2015 as an MP for Ottawa West-Nepean for the Liberal Party and chaired the All-Party Parliamentary Women's Caucus on the Hill from 2015 to 2018.

Women who decide to run for politics should not have to start from scratch.

W omen who decide to run for politics should not have to start from scratch. We should be building on each other's knowledge. Too often, women see political life as limited space, and so we compete with one another in that limited space rather than seeing it as open-ended where we can get in and also help other women to get in.

Before I ran in the 2011 federal election, I managed iknowpolitics.org in New York with a staff on five continents involved in 20 country launches. We had huge online network hosting discussions in four different languages: Spanish, English, French, and Arabic. I launched it in Arabic. iKNOW Politics allows women to not only share tools for campaigns but also to share knowledge on how to navigate the unwritten rules of politics. There are many ways to be an effective parliamentarian. Sharing stories of women who have been through it cuts corners for others coming up behind — especially in developing countries and new democracies.

> *I left that meeting thinking "I can do this!"*

TINA BEAUDRY-MELLOR

Tina Beaudry-Mellor was the Saskatchewan chair of Equal Voice (2013–2015) and was elected to serve as a member in the Legislative Assembly (MLA) for the riding of Regina-University in Saskatchewan in 2016 for the Saskatchewan Party.

At first, I was hunting for workshops for those of us in the early stages of exploring politics. Just before the 2012 municipal election, the YWCA brought together 20 to 30 of us from all party affiliations — and those with none. The YWCA encouraged us to run and offered their support. It was a very empowering event with excellent networking and outreach over coffee, wine, and cheese.

I registered for a campaign school with the Federation of Canadian Municipalities (FCM) and took an online course with Equal Voice. Both were very informative and helped me map my way.

I left that meeting thinking "I can do this!"

> *The first set of networks I reached out to were circles of family, friends, and organizations.*

STEPHANIE MAGHNAM

An active member of the Dunrobin Women's Institute and the Ottawa Muslim Women's Organization, Stephanie Maghnam was the Liberal Party candidate for the Kanata-Carleton riding in the 2018 Ontario provincial election.

Getting up and started took me six months. A big part of that time was contemplation. I had to overcome my own doubts and reassure myself that the things that I stand for in my own community had tremendous value — and that was worth the possibility of losing. This was something I could do well. I saw it as an opportunity to better serve my community and help people, which I had already been doing for a number of years. The first set of networks I reached out to were circles of family, friends, and organizations I already belong to. I spoke with community leaders who inspired me and anyone I knew who would give reassurance that I would be a good representative. I felt the need to ask many people for their opinions and advice. It was like a "kitchen cabinet." Perhaps it delayed me too much, but it was all a part of my journey.

The whole gruelling process of the nomination involved different networks. You're on your own. I built a team with the types of skills I thought we would need at this stage. The team became like a second family as we drove through the intense process of building our membership base and reaching out to as many people as possible. Our hearts became ignited with spreading our vision of what our community is and what it can be.

When I won the nomination, a new circle of support came in. The party now had a stake in me. Party professionals offered input, resources, and advice. The local association was now on the team. Winning the riding was part of the grander goal. MP Karen McCrimmon and Councillor Marianne Wilkinson were marvellous role models and mentors. I should mention media circles too. In Edmonton, Alberta, I had been a reporter before moving to Ottawa. Cultivating relationships with the media was part of the journey too.

The most important network of all was my own family. My husband and kids were at the centre of it all. Without their support, my journey would not have been possible.

SHERRY SENIS

Sherry Senis served on city council in Pickering, Ontario, from 1994 to 1997, where she was the only woman, before moving to the Township of Selwyn. As of 2018, Senis has successfully served for 12 years on Selwyn Township Council with two terms as deputy mayor.

The top advice I would give to anyone running is the absolute importance of networking.

From 1994 to 1997, I served on the council of the town of Pickering. Politics had never been on my radar. Friends encouraged me to run, so I began watching council debates on the local cable station and decided I had something to offer. If I hadn't been asked, I wouldn't have run. It's such a rewarding way to give back to your community. Who wouldn't want to do that?

The top advice I would give to anyone running is the absolute importance of networking. Network, network, network. That's it. Once you network, you can then fundraise and tap into circles of volunteers. Then? Put on your running shoes. The base of any campaign is on the doorstep. People want to see you face-to-face. And I wanted to hear their issues first-hand. Democracy happens on the doorstep. You win your seat one door at a time.

Mentors are important to foster leadership in young women.

IQRA KHALID

Iqra Khalid was elected MP in 2015 for Mississauga-Erin Mills, Ontario, for the Liberal Party. As a student at York University, Khalid was the president of the Pakistani Student Association, media relations ambassador for the York University Student Alumni Association, and communications coordinator for the Council for the Advancement of Muslim Professionals.

Mentors are important to foster leadership in young women. My heritage is from Pakistan, and we have had very prominent Pakistani women to look up to, such as Benazir Bhutto, who was twice elected prime minister of Pakistan before her assassination in 2007 at the age of 35.

Since being elected, I often have South Asian women, and women in general, bringing their daughters towards me saying, "Please mentor her!" Women of colour especially are now looking at politics as a choice that is open to them. Mentors become instrumental in encouraging their confidence.

Personally, before law school, in my undergraduate studies at York University, I had wonderful professors as mentors in my own life.

Getting on the Ballot

The first step, when entering politics, provincially or federally, is securing the party nomination, or "getting on the ballot," which can be a hurdle. The general public is rarely engaged in this part of the democratic process; it happens well before an election and is an internal contest in a party to secure a candidate for its roster for the next election. Generally, the contestant who sells the most party memberships or signs up the most people to the party (depending on party affiliation) and gets out the most votes becomes the candidate. Various election laws and policies govern the raising, spending, and auditing of money involved in the nomination campaign, and donors at this stage of the political process are not entitled to a tax return. In the absence of well-honed political networks and finely tuned nomination skills, women can lose their footing and disappear.

One of my nominations was perhaps typical of what many people face. The nomination was held in a local arena. The noise reached a fever pitch as candidates took to the stage for their last chance to speak to delegates before voting opened. We each had three minutes to make our pitch. When the speeches finished, the balloting opened. Voting was robust. I ended up coming in third. Being the one with the least votes, I fell off the ballot. My ballots were redistributed between the two front runners depending on how people had marked their second preference on my ballots. That's when the strange world of the preferential ballot catapulted the second-place contestant over the first-place one.

THE NOMINATION

There are four important factors at play in a nomination: election laws and policies (which differ at the federal, provincial, and municipal levels), the official political party (federal, provincial, and sometimes municipal), the local party association, and your campaign team. These roles vary greatly throughout the different levels of politics.

1. Canada Elections Act: All elections are governed by election laws or by-laws; abiding by the rules in the election is essential. A breach of election rules can cost you the nomination, while election fraud can put you in jail.

2. Electoral District Association (EDA): The first encounter with the party begins with the candidate search committee run by the local party association, the EDA. The EDA is responsible for suggesting and booking the location for the nomination meeting.

3. Political Party: Political parties decide on the date of the nomination and can delay the date without much warning. Parties can also declare a cut-off date, after which no new party members (or "memberships sold") are eligible to vote at the nomination meeting. At this stage, the party gives the contestant the list of all eligible voters. Moving the date of the nomination meeting and/or changing the cut-off date can affect a contestant's ability to build membership numbers, sustain momentum, and ultimately even win.

4. Campaign Team: Most women interviewed described the indispensable role their families and campaign teams played during their campaign. Some contestants hire campaign managers and open campaign offices, while others rely entirely on volunteers. A campaign team builds a database of supporters and works on get-out-the-vote (GOTV) efforts. The race is won — or lost — depending on how disciplined a campaign team is in implementing its strategy to pull the vote and to persuade those who have not bought their membership from you to consider placing you second on their ballot. There is no absentee voting permitted in nominations.

ROCHELLE SQUIRES

Rochelle Squires was elected MLA for the Progressive Conservative Party of Manitoba for the riding of Riel in 2016. The *Winnipeg Free Press* described her campaign with this headline: "PC candidate wearing out a lot of shoe leather on streets."

My first nomination, I spent a great deal of time getting to know party officials and the local party association. It is important to cultivate party support. It is also important that local riding associations remain neutral in nomination processes to ensure a fair and competitive process.

My second time around, I realized the whole contest should be based on grassroots membership sales. The real value lies in relentless door-to-door selling of memberships. The rules permit younger family members — from 14 years old — to participate. So, behind every door may lie many family members able to vote at a nomination, and even if one member behind the door may not support you, there are other members who may. The real value in contesting a nomination lies in securing grassroots support to win the nomination. I invested my time in my team and on doorsteps.

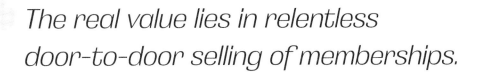

The real value lies in relentless door-to-door selling of memberships.

Most people we spoke with had no idea how the election process worked.

RASHEDA NAWAZ

Rasheda Nawaz is a sustainable community development and climate change consultant who has worked at all three levels of government. Nawaz contested the federal Liberal nomination in Nepean, Ontario, in 2015.

O ur team was outstanding. Countless hours over many months were spent going door to door seeking support, one person or family at a time. We held neighbourhood gatherings to explain the nomination process and convince people to buy memberships.

During this time, we accumulated hundreds of new members in the party. Most people we spoke with had no idea how the election process worked. Only at the time of an election did people become interested in knowing who the candidates were to decide who to vote for. So, our challenge was to explain to people about the nomination process: that one would not be able to vote in selecting a candidate without being a member of the party.

We sold as many memberships as we could. It was very rewarding, but the process was very slow. At the end, we were up against the odds when big batches of sold memberships overtook our local efforts. Parties need to seriously address this issue. If the goal is to increase members and money, that is one thing. But if the aim is to educate and involve citizens and truly encourage women from all sections of society, then the process needs to be rethought.

My running for office was about what I wanted to achieve.

SHERI BENSON

Sheri Benson was elected as the MP for Saskatoon West in 2015 for the NDP. Benson was CEO of the United Way of Saskatoon & Area prior to her election.

T here was already another person in the nomination race. She had run in a previous federal election. My daughter and I had supported her. She was an awesome candidate and a wonderful person. I knew I had to focus on the task of selling memberships, but first I asked myself how I should approach running against someone I knew and respected. I asked myself, "What would I appreciate if I were in her shoes?"

My daughter suggested that I phone her and let her know my intention before telling anybody else. It was a sign of my respect for her. I wanted to let her know why I was running. I've always been so glad I made that difficult decision. It was really who I was.

My running for office was not about beating someone else or disliking the other candidates. My running for office was about what I wanted to achieve. I was driven by my values and a set of issues I knew I could contribute to in a very meaningful manner. I ended up running against someone I knew and admired. I knew I had to explain all that to her.

HELEN WILSON

Helen Wilson, an active participant in her local party riding association, ran for MP in Hamilton Centre, Ontario, for the Liberal Party in 2008; she was also a provincial candidate for Hamilton West in 1990. Wilson was trustee in Ward One for the Hamilton Board of Education from 1991 to 1994.

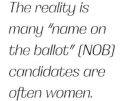

The reality is many "name on the ballot" (NOB) candidates are often women.

I have worked for the party for as long as I can remember and am very committed to their values. When our area did not have a candidate to be on the ballot, I volunteered. It is important for a party to show strength in every riding and every region. I know very well the energy and time campaigns demand. Even being a "name on the ballot" entails significant commitment. It is also the case in politics that surprises happen.

The reality is many "name on the ballot" (NOB) candidates are often women. They are running in unwinnable ridings. Just as soon as the chances for victory in the riding are high, the field becomes flooded with people competing to be the candidate. If you agree to be a NOB, you will gain important experience. And you are contributing to your party and the democratic process. But that all must be weighed in the balance of your family and community commitments.

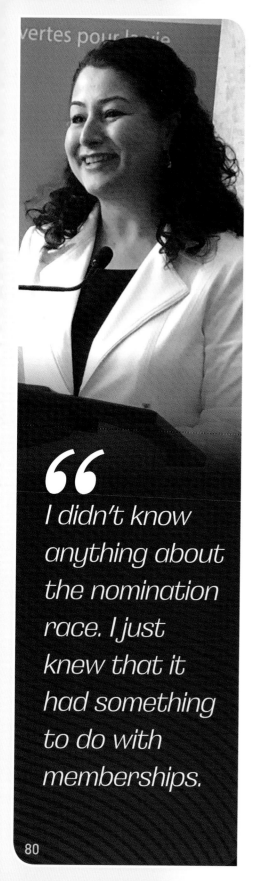

> **"**
> *I didn't know anything about the nomination race. I just knew that it had something to do with memberships.*

MARYAM MONSEF

In 2015, after unsuccessfully running for mayor of Peterborough in 2014, Maryam Monsef was elected as the MP for Peterborough-Kawartha in Ontario for the Liberal Party. Formerly Minister of Democratic Institutions, Monsef was appointed Minister for Women and Gender Equality and Minister of International Development.

I ran first for mayor. I had not even been on city council at the time, but I was asked to contest the incumbent, and that was my first experience. What haunted me from the mayoral race and motivated me to enter the nomination race for the 2015 federal election was the image of the 9879 people who had voted for me for mayor. That was the fire in my belly. These people had invested their hopes in me, and I felt like I had let them down. I carried them everywhere.

I didn't know anything about the nomination race. I just knew that it had something to do with memberships. I had never been part of any party. I never thought of myself as belonging to any party. So, the first step was figuring out which party fit me best. I have always had progressive liberal values. I just didn't realize I was a Liberal.

I also received pragmatic advice to run with the party likely to win. At the time, the NDP and the Liberals were neck and neck, and actually I think the Liberals were slightly behind. I decided to run with a party that not only shared my values but that had a leader that I could relate to. I pictured myself in caucus. I asked myself which leader I could persuade on issues and have the best influence. I also looked at the leader's team. The people coming around Justin Trudeau were from all walks of life, some seasoned professionals and community leaders. That is how I chose the party.

So, I met the executive association, filled out the forms, and went through the process. Then, the selling of memberships began. It was a very tough process and ended up extremely close, being decided by a handful of votes.

HELENA JACZEK

Helena Jaczek was MPP for Oak Ridges-Markham from 2007 to 2018, serving as Minister of Health and Long-Term Care and Minister of Community and Social Services for the Ontario Liberal Party.

At first, I thought I would seek the nomination in the riding of York North in Ontario. At the time, the mayor's son decided to seek the nomination. I remained undeterred. But I underestimated the large family, deep roots, and extensive networks he had. I went door to door selling to friends and families in different neighbourhoods and steadily climbing my sales to 300 memberships. But my competitor had somewhere near three times that, I guessed.

Another riding with which I was associated was open. I assessed the timeline and possibility to sell sufficient memberships there. Being practical, I knew winning nomination races was all about the numbers. After meeting with the other Electoral District Association, I decided to drop out of one race and enter the other. We sold memberships vigorously. It takes flexibility and hard work and, even then, the unexpected can happen. The other contestants in the race dropped out. I ended up acclaimed and became the candidate.

> *It takes flexibility and hard work and, even then, the unexpected can happen.*

For me, a big challenge of entering politics was just ... understanding the process.

TRACY MACCHARLES

Tracy MacCharles served as an MPP in the riding Pickering-Scarborough East from 2011 to 2018. She was appointed to various cabinet positions for the Ontario Liberal Party, including Minister Responsible for Accessibility, Minister Responsible for Women's Issues, and Minister of Children and Youth Services.

For me, a big challenge of entering politics was just getting the information and understanding the process. Being a politician wasn't a lifelong goal. I believed in public and community service. I had worked in the provincial government prior to my private sector career and had volunteered for provincial level boards and councils. When I learned that the incumbent in Pickering-Scarborough East was retiring, I was curious. I grew up in the riding and was raising my family in the riding. I was very involved in the community. Although I shared the values of the Ontario Liberal Party, I didn't have any experience with the political process. I was also recovering from my second bout of cancer.

I set up a "kitchen cabinet" of family and friends. We would wade through the constitutions and rules trying to make sense of it all and meet the timelines. I never felt completely confident. We were always on the journey discovering the system. The nomination to become the candidate for my party was contested, and the five other (male) nomination candidates had what I thought was more and better experience.

In the end, I realized that I was a very good candidate and that I was in the race for all the right reasons. I went on to secure the nomination in June of 2011. I won the general election later that year, taking 47 percent of the vote. I was re-elected in 2014 with 52 percent of the vote.

JEANNETTE CHAU

Jeannette Chau was a Liberal contestant for Mississauga-Erin Mills leading up to the 2015 federal election. Chau used her presence in the race to have an impact on policy debates.

My fellow competitors in the nomination race viewed me as someone they weren't sure of. Though my numbers of sold memberships did not match the thousands which others had sold, I was still a threat. The nomination was by preferential ballot.

They knew that I had a core group and that depending on who I supported, this could make a difference in who was going to finally get elected in the nomination race. So, they were always looking over their shoulder at me and not sure what was going to happen.

> *Though I did not outnumber my fellow competitors on sales, I carried influence by weight of my participation in the race.*

That is the nature of nominations. Though I did not outnumber my fellow competitors on sales, I carried influence by weight of my participation in the race. By force of this influence, I had an impact on the conversation through the issues that I chose to support and the themes I raised during the race. It's not always about winning. Sometimes, the best you can do is exert impact.

DEB SCHULTE

Deb Schulte served from 2010 to 2014 as a regional councillor for Vaughan on York Regional Council before moving to federal politics. In the 2015 federal election, Schulte was elected as the MP for King-Vaughan for the Liberal Party.

My first federal election was in 2015. I had never heard of "The Wall" — the system for pulling out the vote at the nomination meeting — when I was building my team and preparing for a contested nomination. The week before the nomination meeting, it all boiled down to converting our large database of sold memberships into an orderly method of tracking voters as they arrived and cast their votes. I quickly reached out for some training.

A terrific team had invested considerable energy selling memberships, which we felt would position us strongly for the nomination. But we had to convert those lists into a system to deliver the vote. It took several nights and key leaders on the team using big scrolls of paper to map out, neighbourhood by neighbourhood, where our supporters lived and what their coordinates were, so we would be prepared early on E-day to pull the vote.

The night before the nomination, we hung door knockers on all the doors of our supporters to remind people of the location and time of the nomination meeting. I was on the phone non-stop throughout the week personally persuading people to come to the meeting on Saturday.

Very early the next morning, we set up our room at the nomination hall. By nine o'clock, the captains assigned to parts of "The Wall" started texting and phoning all our supporters. Drivers out in the neighbourhoods were on standby to help with transportation. Every single pulled vote counted. Nomination meetings are often won and lost by single digits. All the effort came down to delivering the vote on that one day.

RUTH ELLEN BROSSEAU

Ruth Ellen Brosseau was asked by the NDP to put her name on the ballot in the 2011 election for Berthier-Maskinongé in Quebec — to her surprise, she won. In the subsequent 2015 election, Brosseau increased her vote share and returned as an MP for a second term. She was appointed NDP caucus chair in 2016, NDP House Leader in 2018, and NDP Whip in 2019.

I was working on the university campus. As a single mom, my priority was my son and the support of my parents. Universities are filled with lots of politics and debates. I was part of that whole scene and enjoyed the whole environment. When the federal election was approaching, some of the NDP club members on campus asked me about running as a candidate. There were some ridings still open.

It was a world away from what I had ever considered. I had a vacation long-planned with my son, which would preclude my being present during much of the campaign. But the party assessed the context and invited me to put my name on the ballot.

I am likely one of the better-known paper candidates. I was on that vacation when the call came that I had won. It was an enormous challenge and privilege. I threw myself into the task and spent most of the first months doing little except meeting all my constituents in a determined effort to be a credible and effective member of Parliament. One election cycle later, my re-election was a great honour and gave me the reassurance and confidence that I was succeeding in providing a strong local voice for my constituents in the House of Commons. Mine was a most unlikely path into politics.

Mine was a most unlikely path into politics.

The Campaign Trail

When you win the nomination, you become your party's official candidate. The last day of the nomination race is the first day of the campaign. A thank-you speech at the nomination meeting is also a rallying call to delegates in attendance. Feelings run high in nominations; it's not always easy to forge a united team on the spot. But soon enough, you become part of the party brand, and the campaign begins to "deliver the riding" for the party.

Time is tight, and with thousands of voters to meet, canvassing teams fan out across the riding in the dash to be on the doorstep of as many voters as possible. Walking up to a stranger's door doesn't come naturally to most people. Yet canvassing is the cornerstone of every campaign — candidates get the chance to meet people in the places where they live and hear their issues face to face.

During one of my campaigns, Ralph Goodale visited the riding and gave me advice about canvassing decisions. I've never forgotten his words: "When you're fishing, go to the fish pond."

So, where are the fish? Look at the history of party support over several elections, poll by poll; it becomes apparent where the strongest support is consistently located. In these polls, a candidate canvass, accompanied by a literature drop and phone outreach, can consolidate a solid base of candidate support. In contrast, there are polls where the party rarely wins. Polls in between these two are the swing polls. Consolidating support in polls where the party is traditionally popular and then moving to the swing polls maximizes both the candidate's and the canvassers' energy and time.

Women running for municipal council, for First Nations leadership, or for the leadership of a political party have different dynamics on the campaign trail.

WOMEN AT THE HELM

Not every woman needs to run to be a party candidate to be meaningfully involved in politics. During the 2015 federal election, Anna Gainey was president of the Liberal Party and Rebecca Blaikie was president of the NDP. In this election, also, three women, Anne McGrath, Jenni Byrne, and Katie Telford, held the top roles running the national campaigns of Canada's major political parties. While it was assumed that "winning the women's vote" was an important ingredient of success, putting women at the top of campaign structures was not a given — it was a first. McGrath, Byrne, and Telford raised the profile of women and brought national attention to the pivotal and important role women play in national campaigns.

| Anna Gainey | Rebecca Blaikie | Anne McGrath | Jenni Byrne | Katie Telford |

PEGGY SATTLER

Peggy Sattler, first elected in a by-election in 2013, found herself at the centre of attention as she transitioned into the party candidate for the NDP in London West, Ontario.

From the first campaign photo, you become a brand.

Because we were in a by-election, the party had really poured a lot of resources into the campaign. In a by-election, volunteers arrive from across the province. You've got cheques being sent and multiple phone banks working for you at a distance. You can really pull out all the stops.

I had had a professional career; I was director of policy at a research firm and had a professional wardrobe. But I was not in the habit of wearing makeup on a daily basis and had to start. It was one of the small things I grappled with as the party arranged for professional photography for a standard head-and-shoulders shot. From the first campaign photo, you become a brand with a certain kind of look. It's kind of depersonalizing in a way, but I understood the party drive to use the brand to advance its presence in the riding.

CATHERINE MCKENNA

Catherine McKenna was elected as the MP for Ottawa-Centre in 2015 for the Liberal Party and was appointed Minister of Environment and Climate Change.

> *I think that often campaigns take volunteers for granted and don't engage them properly.*

I just knew I had a problem engaging volunteers because people really wanted to get involved, but we had difficulty calling them all back, engaging them, and rewarding them. We were flat out and barely surviving. I didn't yet have a model.

The chair of my nomination race was having a baby, so I needed to change management for the federal election. I was at a training session where I heard Karin McNair talking about volunteers. She said that private sector principles apply; you need to have expectations, job descriptions, and rewards. I think that often campaigns take volunteers for granted and don't engage them properly; they just hope the volunteers will continue to come. I asked her if she was available to manage a campaign. She had just moved to Ottawa from Toronto, where she had been the president of the Parkdale-High Park riding association. We went out for lunch, and I really had to court her. I said, "I need you to run my campaign because I need someone who understands how to pull this all together." Up went the team posters and in came the model to manage volunteers. She was very focused and professional. The party was advancing the Obama snowflake concept working with neighbourhood teams, but you need ranks of volunteers to get to that stage.

THE SNOWFLAKE MODEL

Barack Obama's team adopted the "snowflake model" for his campaign to become the 44th president of the United States in 2008. Campaigns that use the snowflake model, a method of organizing, focus on the development and empowerment of neighbourhood teams around a central campaign organizer. The campaign organizer appoints team leaders, or captains, who take charge of recruiting volunteers and leading campaigns in their neighbourhood. The resulting organizational structure resembles a snowflake. The campaigns are standardized, but the snowflake model mobilizes grassroots leadership and allows for sustained momentum.

YVONNE JONES

Yvonne Jones, of Inuit ancestry, was a Liberal member of the House of Assembly (MHA) for Cartwright-L'Anse au Clair from 1996 to 2013 and then was elected MP for the riding of Labrador in Newfoundland and Labrador in a by-election in May 2013 and re-elected in 2015.

If I was going to represent this riding, I had to meet people where they lived and hear their concerns personally.

There was no other way. If I was going to represent this riding, I had to meet people where they lived and hear their concerns personally. I took to the road, the air, and even a snowmobile to visit each community across Labrador until I could convince myself that I understood, at a granular level, what people were living day to day. It was the only way I felt I could ask them for their vote.

As an MP, I have opened three constituency offices. We also run rotating clinics. Some people just can't drive the distances it would require if I had only one office. It matters. If I intend to represent people, I have to meet them where they live.

ELIZABETH MAY

Elizabeth May, leader of the Green Party of Canada, and MP for Saanich-Gulf Islands, BC, received simple campaigning tips from two friends: former Prime Minister Paul Martin and physicist, educator, and social activist Ursula Franklin.

Paul Martin gave me a valuable tip on campaigning one day: "You just get an egg timer. You put it in front of you. You don't talk to anyone more than three minutes. Pick up the phone, let the egg timer run, then hang up when the timer rings, and start all over. Start on the list, and continuously make calls. And keep the egg timer at your elbow." I never forgot the egg timer.

Ursula Franklin was a dear friend of mine. I quote her a lot in my book *How to Save the World in Your Spare Time*. One of the things she used to say is that a potluck supper is women's way of organizing. No one has to do all the work. A potluck supper is never over-organized, yet somehow it all comes together. You get a nice distribution of salads, main dishes, and desserts. Somehow, it all just happens. Everybody shares, and there are leftovers for the host. In a lot of ways, in my campaigns, I like to organize with Ursula's potluck supper metaphor in mind.

You just get an egg timer. You put it in front of you. You don't talk to anyone more than three minutes.

LINDA DUNCAN

Linda Duncan, NDP, was the only non-Conservative MP elected in Alberta in the 2008 federal election; she went on to win her seat again in 2011 and 2015.

> *It matters to me to understand issues directly from the doorstep.*

We used neighbourhood teams and were deeply committed to very grassroots mobilization of support. We canvassed block by block and neighbourhood by neighbourhood, engaging people and volunteers on their street blocks.

It matters to me to understand issues directly from the doorstep and to engage people as personally as possible in getting them out to vote. We took detailed organizational time to assign campaigns to neighbourhoods. I wanted to be present in them all. It matters to me that people knew I was taking their voice to Ottawa.

LINDA SLAVIN

Linda Slavin has run in Peterborough, Ontario, at all three levels of government, including provincially and federally for the NDP. With her experience, Slavin has helped mobilize countless campaigns and assisted many candidates making the transition from nomination contestant to party candidate.

> *In elections, ... it is the party brand and leader who now enter the equation and carry the riding.*

The luxury of the nomination race for contestants is that you are speaking to people who know the policies. They understand what's at stake in terms of their party locally and nationally. You're talking to people who've been through this before, so it's quite a different message they want to hear. They want to know that you know your stuff. They want to know that you can communicate it. They want to know that you're honest and agreeable. You're really selling yourself. They are asking themselves at this stage, "Can this person represent the party and win the riding for us?"

This all changes when you become the official party candidate. Now, you're speaking to a much wider audience. Your message has to reach across the entire community, many of whom may not know [the party's] policies. In elections, your message is much more broadly cast, and it is the party brand and leader who now enter into the equation and carry the riding. You are the party instrument locally.

LINDA REID

Linda Reid was elected MLA for Richmond East for the BC Liberal Party in 1991 and went on to become the longest-serving woman in the BC Legislature. Reid was elected Speaker of the Legislative Assembly in 2013 and served as the chair of the Commonwealth Women Parliamentarians Canada Region (2014–2017).

Surround yourself with people who are prepared to disagree with you. You need the breadth of opinion. Diversity on the team is so important. If everybody agrees with you, you don't have the right people on your team. You need an accountant, a lawyer, a humanitarian, a social worker, and NGO leaders, who understand all the different layers that you find in a community. Then, make sure that you follow the rules of the election process so that you don't get disqualified. Your accountant and lawyer and official agents are key. You may have the best ideas in the world, but they could all end with a misstep. Make sure you have the best talent you can find on board.

I love elections. I think they're absolutely exhilarating. You get to talk to people every single day about what matters to them. Then you can craft your approach to public policy based on the input you receive. Nothing better. I do door knocking year in, year out, month in, month out. I say to women entering politics, "If you don't enjoy meeting people, perhaps this is not the choice for you."

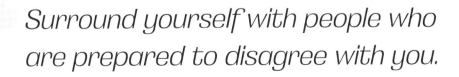

Surround yourself with people who are prepared to disagree with you.

It took close to two and a half hours to make it from one end of the riding to the other.

BARB JINKERSON

Barb Jinkerson ran for MPP for the Ontario Liberal Party in the rural riding of Hastings-Peterborough in the 1995 Ontario election.

It took close to two and a half hours to make it from one end of the riding to the other. I consumed a lot of gas and took a great deal of time to make it to events spread from one town to another. Fortunately, I had friends from my church spread around the whole riding, so I could make it to a kitchen table no matter what town I was in. There was always an invitation to stay overnight in a spare bedroom during the campaign.

We live on a beef farm, and my husband is in the farm equipment business, so I heard lots of stories over lots of suppers. You need to be aware of milking time and harvest time. Farmers are busy people, but they always make time — and a pie! I leaned on my church family and the kindness of so many to knock on doors in every corner of the riding. That's what is entailed for a candidate running in a rural riding.

I knew that if you knocked on enough doors ... you could win.

SYLVIA SUTHERLAND

Sylvia Sutherland ran at all three levels of government: federally in 1980 and provincially in 1995, both as a Liberal candidate, and municipally in the 1980s and 1990s. She twice served as mayor of Peterborough (1986–1991, 1998–2006).

When we moved to Norwood from Toronto, I was approached to run for village council. I had worked on a Liberal campaign in Toronto for Paul Hellyer, so I knew the outline of a campaign. I knew that if you knocked on enough doors — in those days there was no social media — you could win. I've always believed in "foot power." Shoe leather is still the most important ingredient of success in campaigns.

YVETTE BIONDI

Yvette Biondi served as a school board trustee for the Sainte-Croix School Board in Quebec from 1990 to 1994 and served as a city councillor in the City of Saint-Laurent from 1994 to 2002.

Women generally don't pay enough attention to developing a network of contacts who will mobilize support during an election campaign. Single moms certainly don't have the same time for building support networks. Their time off is often focused on healthy meals for the children and their school activities. That's why women are often in a weaker position — especially single moms.

Campaigning and neighbourhood canvassing are foundational to democracy. I needed to hear the issues on the doorstep and take those issues to council. Campaigning door to door, I was advised to wear black and fit into the image of the other (male) candidates. I chose yellow — bright yellow.

The life of a single mother as a representative on the political stage is an experience full of traps and pitfalls as well as amazing rewards. I hadn't the same financial resources and certainly not the contacts available as my male colleagues. But I had a dream. As an American musician has said, "If you don't have a dream, you will never have a dream come true."

I was advised to wear black and fit into the image of the other (male) candidates. I chose yellow — bright yellow.

PAT CARNEY

In 1980, Pat Carney was the first woman elected as an MP for Vancouver Centre. Re-elected in 1984, Carney held three cabinet posts for the Progressive Conservative Party: Minister of Energy, Mines and Resources, Minister of International Trade, and president of the Treasury Board — the first woman to hold these senior economic cabinet positions.

Former Tory cabinet minister Flora MacDonald would be delighted that Prime Minister Stephen Harper called the federal election on the day of her funeral. She was a formidable campaigner. Sometimes she gave speeches in place of former shy Conservative candidate Margaret Mary Macdonald. She told me nobody in the audience knew the difference.

I was equally shy in my first campaign in Vancouver Centre, horrified that I was expected to accost perfect strangers in shopping malls. So, Flora came west to teach me campaign techniques. Dragging me along behind her, she would beam at people and say, "I want you to meet your Conservative candidate in Vancouver Centre." People beamed back. Everybody knew Flora.

When she went back to her Kingston riding, my volunteers and I went to the busiest street corner in the riding. For my first attempt, I chose an elderly lady with curly grey hair and a cane who was crossing the street. When she reached the curb, I stuck out my hand and said bravely, "I'm Pat Carney, your Conservative candidate, and I need your vote."

The benign-appearing senior drew back her hand and snapped, "I would rather my hand withered and dropped off before shaking hands with a Conservative" and walked away. Stunned, I put my shunned hand back in my pocket. I tell this story in my book *Trade Secrets*, and it brings me a smile every time. But I did learn to enjoy campaigning and was elected twice in the riding before retiring.

My volunteers and I went to the busiest street corner in the riding.

I decided that if I didn't know the answer, I would say so.

HEATHER WATSON

Heather Watson's foray into electoral politics was eight years in the making. She was first asked to volunteer on a mayoralty campaign in 2010; she announced her bid for councillor in 2018. Watson now serves as Douro Ward Councillor in Douro-Dummer Township.

In the past, there had not been much interest in the municipal election as most candidates had been acclaimed in recent years. There were three of us newcomers who were contesting long-standing incumbents. I was the only woman and was generations younger than the others. There were two all-candidates meetings, both of which were standing room only. There was a definite interest in community engagement of this nature.

I had heard lots about Betsy's "yellow sail" technique to keep a sharp focus. But it was sometimes hard to keep on track when things popped up and well-intended people tried to pull you off course. I set my sights on a positive campaign message and refused to get embroiled in some misogynistic messaging happening on social media. I had a campaign to win.

Debate questions were emailed to the moderator but not shared with candidates ahead of the meeting. I decided that if I didn't know the answer, I would say so. I would tell people the principles I would apply to any issue in general, then ask for that person's contact to reach out to them after the meeting when I had formulated an informed answer.

Some incumbents took shots at me. I took that as a compliment, but it was baffling to me because I was running for a different ward seat — we weren't even competitors. There was definitely a feeling of the old guard sticking together, and I was putting them all on the defensive. My campaign theme was to anchor in community tradition but welcome fresh change. It resonated with people as I connected with them at the door. They echoed that it was time for some new energy. I never stopped canvassing throughout the entire online voting period. I campaigned right up to the end of E-day. The next chapter began the night of E-day. I was elected councillor, and the road in elected office now lay ahead!

SHARMILA SETARAM

Sharmila Setaram works as a human resources consultant for the Ontario Clean Water Agency. Setaram is the former president of the Board of Directors at Amnesty International Canada. In 2018, she ran for city councillor in Mississauga.

It was a thrill to run for the first time in Ward 1 for Mississauga's city council. I am a racialized woman. In our city, about 57.2 percent of citizens identify as racialized, but we are not visible in city council. Yet decisions rendered by city council impact very heavily on our lives: housing, transportation, job opportunities, education ... and the list goes on.

During our last all-candidates debate, we were invited at the last minute to put up a campaign sign on the wall. The space was limited, so I chose to hang a smaller sign. The male candidates used their large signs, and one of them covered part of my sign, effectively reducing my name from Sharmila to Harmila. I was shocked that he would put his sign in such a way that it would cover part of my name. Another candidate brought it to my attention, and I had to divert my energy and go into troubleshooting mode to resolve the issue while 100+ citizens watched.

I had to divert my energy and go into troubleshooting mode to resolve the issue while 100+ citizens watched.

Running for Leadership

Running for leadership of a political party, Band Council, or the Assembly of First Nations is a challenge, but it is a challenge several women in this book have undertaken for a number of reasons and under a number of circumstances.

Some women who ran for leadership were not in elected office when the opportunity to run arose; their filing of papers to run for leadership took the media, and likely many political observers, by surprise. Karen McCrimmon speaks about this experience in her 2013 federal Liberal leadership race. In other cases, the chance to run for leadership was triggered by the resignation of a party leader. Nicole Sarauer, in Saskatchewan, describes the circumstances that led to her becoming party leader.

The campaign team for a leadership race is a crucial component of a leadership run. The team must span the province or country and must understand your vision. Niki Ashton knew she would face gender-specific hurdles and critiques. She wanted her team to be fully forewarned and in tune with her feminist philosophy as they managed her campaign. Elizabeth May built her team based on national networks from her life of advocacy for the environment.

All the women were convinced that their participation was important to changing the conversation, adding depth and a different dimension to debates. And all the women knew the demands on their time and the challenge of money would be extraordinary. All were crystal clear on their motive for running. All ran to win.

LISA RAITT

Lisa Raitt, MP for Halton (2008–2015) and Milton (2015) for the Conservative Party, became Deputy Leader of the Official Opposition in 2017, following her appointments as Minister of Natural Resources, Minister of Labour, and Minister of Transport.

If you're going to go, make your decision quickly.

I went through an intense decision-making process evaluating whether to run for leadership of the Ontario Conservative Party. On January 25, 2018, party leader Patrick Brown resigned amid issues whirling around his conduct. The party named an interim leader, then announced its intentions to hold a leadership race to elect a permanent leader ahead of the June 2018 provincial election. I had to decide swiftly.

It's not necessary that you're going to say yes all the time. My decision was evidence-driven. First, provincial politics is a completely different culture [from federal]. Federal Conservatives and provincial Conservatives may have joint memberships, but they're not the same party at all. Assessing this cultural difference was an important ingredient in my decision. The second element of my decision was to assess whether I had the two building blocks that would be needed for the leadership race: a top-notch organization familiar with the Ontario system and the money to pay immediately, upfront, for people to work on my campaign.

After looking at both those things in the very quick time available to announce my decision, I weighed the evidence. I asked myself what purpose I would serve in the party and in the debates other than flat-out winning. The only purpose I could have, I felt, was to win the leadership and help the party in a time of turmoil. If I didn't win, there would be no purpose to my being there, and I couldn't hire myself and my colleagues back to the federal level. Those were the elements of my analysis. I weighed the evidence, then slept on it overnight. It took one good night's sleep. Then I announced I would not run. It's not always about saying yes.

My decision to run for the federal leadership was within another context. It came down to an analysis of skills and timing. I knew I had the skills. These were recognized subsequently when leader Andrew Scheer appointed me to be the Deputy Leader of the party. Any party must put forward candidates Canadians trust, candidates Canadians can identify with, and candidates Canadians believe understand their issues. That's what I knew I could bring to the table.

Then swiftly came the challenge of finding the time, the money, the people, and the organization. That's what took me a little bit longer until I arrived at my final decision to run. I jumped in, but I was too late. At the end of the day, by the time I got into the race, people who would naturally have supported me had already gone to other candidates. That was my lesson. If you're going to go, make your decision quickly.

Oddly enough, I felt like I was everybody's mother or big sister in the field of 13 candidates. Before going onstage for a debate, I would be talking to everybody, trying to make things calm and easy. During the debate, when I saw somebody unnecessarily attack another person, I would do what I could to calm the waters. When I thought somebody was going over the line, I would vocalize that as well. So, I had a very different role within the leadership race.

My place in the debates was to raise issues that I knew mattered and needed to be in the dialogue; I wanted to speak for moms of kids with autism, caregivers, and women over 60. It can't always be about taxes, markets, and free trade. There needs to be space in national debates on the social and human side of our national vision. It isn't all about the money. In the end, I viewed the whole federal leadership race as a positive experience.

Leadership must be something you're passionate about. For me, it was in my core.

NIKI ASHTON

MP for Churchill-Keewatinook Aski in Manitoba, Niki Ashton announced her bid for leadership of the federal NDP in 2017. Ashton was first elected MP in 2008 at the age of 26.

The process of saying yes to a leadership race is very similar to the process of saying yes to a nomination. Only the magnitude of it is bigger. Leadership must be something you're passionate about. For me, it was in my core.

There is an obvious gendered approach to running for leadership.

It's very important to have a strong core team that knows you well. I also think it is important to have a core team that has a feminist analysis and recognizing that, as women, it will be harder to raise money. The campaign will have to deal with sexism on social media and in mainstream media. Politically, you need a team that knows it will be tougher for a woman and put support systems in place. You need to vent and have a response team that a man running for leadership might not need.

As women, many of us are overly cautious. We need everything in place before we take bold steps. Barriers can loom large. But, at some point, you just have to go for it. Men seem to do it all the time. But I think as women we have to sometimes let go of overplanning and forget plan B. If we intend to reach parity, let's get moving.

KAREN MCCRIMMON

Karen McCrimmon was in the Canadian Forces for 31 years. Despite losing her first campaign for Parliament in 2011, she entered the Liberal Party leadership race in 2013. When Justin Trudeau won the leadership, McCrimmon turned her attention to the 2015 federal campaign, running successfully to represent the riding of Kanata-Carleton.

I wanted to excite people about a fresh new leadership model.

I wanted to excite people about a fresh new leadership model. I wanted to confront the dark arts of slander and spin and negative advertising using so much money. I knew I could bring a fresh leadership style.

I had a career devoted to my country. I would be a tough target for any negative ads. Attacking a woman military veteran would not work. Perhaps that would truncate this escalating negativity in politics. I wanted to change the channel. We had a wonderful slate of leadership candidates. I knew together we could take politics to a higher level. I knew I had the credibility and leadership experience to do just that. So, while my brain was saying, "Are you out of your mind running for leadership?" my heart was saying, "You need to do this." And the truth is, in my entire life, my only regrets have been when I did not pay attention to my heart.

The federal party leadership race in 2013 was six months full throttle. I became addicted to adrenaline. Every day was full of adrenaline. Seven days a week, six months flat out. Then, suddenly, it was over. Justin Trudeau emerged as the party leader, and it all began for him. For the rest of us, it was over in an instant. I went cold turkey.

I think many women might ask at the time of their defeat, "What's wrong with me?" I want women to know my experience. In my view, there's nothing wrong with you. It's perfectly normal. You were addicted to adrenaline. Now, you don't have it anymore. A military medical friend said to me, "You were on some pretty pure drugs, ma'am!" So be prepared, and do not doubt yourself in your exhaustion and recovery. It is part of the cost of a high-stakes political path.

My biggest ditch after the leadership race was the debt I incurred. It took me probably 15 months of really hard work to pay it off. At the time, I regretted running. Sometimes I was sick to my stomach about the debt. It meant a great deal to me when Bob Rae offered his praise saying, "Karen set the example for leadership when she was in the race." So, even though it hurt trying to pay off that debt, in the end, it was worth the cost.

NICOLE SARAUER

Nicole Sarauer was first elected as a trustee. In 2016, she ran for the provincial legislature, winning a seat for the Saskatchewan NDP. In 2017, when the NDP provincial leader stepped down, she was appointed interim leader, the first woman to lead the party in Saskatchewan. She held the role until Ryan Meili was elected leader in 2018.

From the time I was elected in 2016 [as an MLA in the Saskatchewan Legislature], I was getting a push to run for the permanent leadership of the Saskatchewan NDP. I wasn't particularly interested at the time. The amount of work it would take to run a very strong campaign was a big consideration. When interim leader Trent Wotherspoon stepped down, there was a narrow time frame to decide. Caucus was going to vote on who would be Leader of the Opposition and interim leader of the Saskatchewan NDP. It was a matter of a few days. I decided I had value to bring to the table.

What I had to offer was a little different from what other people were offering. I was working with more marginalized people in our community. I was young and newer to the party. I felt I could offer a real sense of renewal and excitement. I knew I could provide a stark contrast to the premier. So, I made the pitch to my colleagues. I leaned in, summoned up my courage, and declared myself a candidate for leadership.

I leaned in, summoned up my courage, and declared myself a candidate for leadership.

I was quite surprised and honoured to be chosen. It was a steep learning curve. Winning the MLA seat and becoming party leader brought a level of exposure and responsibility I was not prepared for until it happened. It was an incredible opportunity to be at the ground level shaping policy. I knew what a privilege it was to speak on behalf of my constituents and others in Saskatchewan who felt left out. It was very humbling. Many people tell you their challenges. To have somebody trust you enough with their story is humbling.

The level of exposure can be overwhelming. You need to make yourself vulnerable. You may not feel comfortable at times. Just because some people might say, "You're too young" or "You don't fit a particular mould," don't think you can't do it. You are just as qualified as anybody else, and there are plenty of people running who are just as doubtful. So, why should you doubt yourself? My exposure level has been much higher than when I was an MLA. The level of activity on social media increased exponentially. Not everybody is going to like you. Be sure of your principles because your popularity will be a roller coaster.

ELIZABETH MAY

For me, this was a partisan fight that had to be fought on partisan turf.

Elizabeth May successfully ran for the leadership of the Green Party of Canada in 2006. In the 2011 federal election, May became the first Green Party candidate to be elected to the House of Commons; she represented the BC riding of Saanich-Gulf Islands. In the 2015 federal election, May had to fight to be part of national televised debates among national party leaders.

The determining factor in my career path has always been to achieve maximum impact on the issues that are the driving force in my life. I left my contract working on Parliament Hill as a lawyer in a minister's office to become executive director of Canada's Sierra Club. I felt the Sierra Club was an important mobilizer in Canada and opinion leader in national debates. But when Mr. Harper became prime minister, any hopes for progressive climate change policies sank, and funding for environmental NGOs fell into jeopardy. The charitable status of many NGOs was threatened. No one would be able to speak out. For me, this was a partisan fight that had to be fought on partisan turf.

I had received many phone calls from friends in the Green Party. A leadership race was planned. One candidate had declared. They wanted a second candidate and a contested race. But the decision to run for leadership of the Green Party was not one I would have taken without my daughter's support. I remember telling her, "I'm afraid, sweetheart; it might mean that I work hard." She replied, "Mom, you work hard 24/7 now; it can't get worse." Of course, it got much worse. I took the chance, resigned from the Sierra Club, and ran for leadership. The decision to enter politics and run for leadership was entirely around public education and fighting for the environment to avert the profound consequences if we ignored it.

Three women drove the campaign: Adriane Carr, Sharon Labchuk, and Catherine Johannson. We ran a flat, non-hierarchical campaign bolstered by contacts in every province selling memberships and fundraising. It was much like a nomination but taken to a national scale. Within the Green Party, as with many parties I imagine, there was already an entrenched hierarchy. I was a newcomer. I hadn't been a member long while most of the men had a history in the party and were supporting the other candidate, an established councillor at Ottawa City Hall. It was an old boys' network. Their campaign was very strong. It was interesting to me how immediately a non-hierarchical culture of trust prevailed in our campaign. We worked our networks and just plain grunted it out to the finish.

It was a tough race, but, in the end, we won on the first ballot with over 60 percent of the convention. That's what a remarkable team can achieve.

AUDREY MCLAUGHLIN

Audrey McLaughlin ran in a by-election and won a seat in Parliament in 1987 for the NDP. McLaughlin won the NDP party leadership race two years later in 1989 and was the first woman in Canada to lead a national party.

I had a lot of people who encouraged me and who were supportive of me — people like Stanley Knowles, whom I really respected. I had lots of people organizing and helping. That's necessary. But it's challenging.

Leadership commands your full attention all the time.

As party leader, you're responsible for far more people than your constituency. You still have your constituency responsibilities, but you now also operate on a national level for the party. So, you're adding, you're not dropping anything. You are adding to your constituency and legislative roles representing citizens, the leadership of a national party, and the mobilization of candidates. It's physically extremely demanding. Leadership commands your full attention all the time. Your mind expands, but your body contracts. You need to be physically and mentally prepared for the rigour.

LYN MCLEOD

Lyn McLeod was first elected to the Ontario Legislature in 1987 for the Ontario Liberal Party and was appointed Minister of Colleges and Universities. Following a cabinet shuffle, she was also named Minister of Energy and Minister of Natural Resources. In 1992, McLeod became the first woman to lead a political party in Ontario.

I needed to be persuaded to run for leadership. I knew that I'd been competent as a cabinet minister, but I needed to be sure I had the fire in the belly and vision to bring to the leadership role. It took people who knew me well to persuade me to bring my values and beliefs about government to the race. Highly centralized governments tend to be somewhat divorced from the reality of needs of people in different regions of Ontario. I ran my campaign as "One size does not fit all." I believed we needed to have government from the bottom up, more responsive to the needs of people. When I ran for leadership, there had not been many women in leadership roles in Canada. There were few images of women leaders and many stereotypes about what women could and could not do. I loved the T-shirt of the time: "A Woman's Place is in the House of Commons." It's important to shift the image of the Fathers of Confederation to filling up the picture with more women leaders.

> *It's important to shift the image of the Fathers of Confederation to filling up the picture with more women leaders.*

Being a party leader? Be prepared. There's no question. The public exposure of a party leader is hugely demanding. I was the Opposition Leader. You don't get any attention until you do something outrageous or the government is under attack for something outrageous — and one or the other has lost credibility. It is a tough, demanding role.

JOYCE MURRAY

Joyce Murray represented the riding of New Westminster in the BC Legislature from 2001 to 2005 and has represented Vancouver Quadra as an MP since 2008 for the Liberal Party. Murray entered the race for Liberal Party leader in 2015; she has since been appointed president of the Treasury Board and Minister of Digital Government in 2019.

I had a clear vision to promote, and I plunged in.

Entering the federal leadership race in November 2012 was part of a continuum for me. When I first ran politically, I didn't know what I was dealing with. It was quite terrifying to take that first leap into politics. Even though I was aware intellectually of the undertaking, it was so different from anything I had ever done in the private sector. That was part of my personal voyage and challenge. It was very rich in learning. Part of me was saying this is the last thing I wanted to do. Another part was saying a strong yes — this is for me!

The same thing happened in the leadership race. I had been in the public eye. I had been a cabinet minister. Yet there was still a sense of terror at that next level of public visibility. I heard my inner voice saying, "Who does she think she is?" I was judging myself. At the same time, I had a very strong conviction that I wanted to be talking about sustainability, climate change, and the overall global environmental challenge. I felt these were national priorities, and I could bring significant experience to leadership. So, it was that same mixture of terror holding me back, with a moral imperative urging me on.

Once I was into the project, the terror was gone. That initial barrier of fear of doing something brand new disappeared. The potential to completely fail had to be stared down. Self-doubt and questioning — "Am I up to the challenge?" — were self-imposed brakes. One candidate, Justin Trudeau, was the candidate everyone considered would win, and indeed he did. But the Liberals wanted real challengers and lively policy debates to build a vigorous party future.

I had run a business and been an MP and a cabinet minister. I felt I could inject solid issues into leaders' debates. I had a clear vision to promote, and I plunged in.

KELLY LAROCCA

Kelly LaRocca was elected Chief of the Mississaugas of Scugog Island
First Nation in 2013 and has served on the elected council since 2008. In
2016, LaRocca was elected Eastern Director for the First Nations Lands
Advisory Board.

It was a very difficult decision to me because I had worked with
my council for many years. Many were surprised when I decided
to make the move and run for Chief. There were hurt feelings. It
did take a toll on our dynamic. However, we all understood I had the
right to run for whatever electoral position I chose. The decision was
very much a family decision. I could not have done the work without
my husband. He took paternal leave and was in my office, which I
basically converted to a nursery. There he was, napping and playing
with our baby.

I spent a lot of time on my election speech to make sure it was true
to my feelings and honoured the former leadership. I wanted to pay
tribute to each of the leaders of the community as I had experienced
their leadership. Each of us has our own strengths, and we are needed
at different times for different reasons. It just flowed naturally that the
experiences I had from school were needed. We were in the middle of
heavy negotiations, and I could focus on these types of issues.

When I made the decision to run for Chief, I could not show any
kind of hesitation because it couldn't work that way. The community
needed to have confidence in my choice to run. Although there were
hurt feelings, I believe the former Chief knew that it was time for the
shift, and she ended up coming back as a councillor. The transition
was difficult as we basically switched spots. She was very dignified
with the results of the election. I was very appreciative. She taught me
a lot, and I wanted to show all councillors my respect. Keeping unity is
important in a small community, especially a First Nations community.

Each of us has our own strengths, and we are needed at different times for different reasons.

> *It's not only what you stand for in politics; it's the way you do politics.*

LIBBY DAVIES

Libby Davies, one of the most experienced MPs in the NDP caucus, declined to run for party leadership in 2011 even though she had filled many leadership roles during her six terms in Parliament, including NDP House Leader and Deputy Leader.

Jack Layton, when he became leader of Canada's NDP at the end of 2003, asked me to be his House Leader. I replied, "Uh, no. I don't think so. I can't do that. I don't know how the House works all that well." Jack basically said, "I don't care about that. You'll learn. I trust you. That's what I want — someone I trust and someone who's not going to play games. I want someone who's going to be upfront and work in an open, transparent way." Jack was looking for qualities.

Leadership wasn't something I asked for. My natural tendency is to find common ground and build consensus. I am a mediator. I believe strongly in issues. I'm a strong advocate for social justice. I was never one who took political sides for the sake of partisanship. I never had enemies. For me, it has always been about the issues.

That non-partisan culture came through in my municipal background. Jack and I shared this quality. We knew each other for years. He was an activist in Toronto, and I was an activist in Vancouver. It was not a matter of rolling over. No, we fought tooth and nail for the people.

For some people, it's all about win or lose. It's about crushing their opposition. It's all about winning. It's like a sports game. That never works for me. For me, it is always about the issues. The reputation I gained was only that. I was fair and constructive with colleagues. I never sought out positions of political leadership. They just happened to me.

Here is my advice to women entering politics: It's not only what you stand for in politics; it's the way you do politics.

DELIA OPEKOKEW

Delia Opekokew was the first Indigenous lawyer ever called to the bar in Ontario in 1979. From Canoe Lake Cree First Nation, she was admitted to the Saskatchewan Bar in 1983. Opekokew ran unsuccessfully for Grand Chief of the Assembly of First Nations at the 1994 leadership convention.

I always saw the issues from the community needs. There were so many major challenges. I looked at the whole issue of wellness, health among Aboriginal people, and I became very, very concerned about the dysfunction, the abuse of substances, the damaged families on the reserve communities. This was about 1990. When I went to the Assembly of First Nations conference in 1994, I knew what needed to be done at the community level. I remember coming back, working out on the treadmill, and thinking to myself, "Someone has to speak to what is needed in the community, and I think I know what it is. I think I'm going to run for the AFN." That's how I decided.

To be nominated, the rules state you need at least 31 Chiefs or proxies, 31 people who were eligible to vote, to sign your nomination papers. So, I did have to spend a lot of time getting a nominator and a seconder. My nominator was my own Chief of Canoe Lake. In fact, we had just finished doing treaty work together. He was Chief for about 25 years. I was honoured to have my home community Chief totally supporting me.

" I knew what needed to be done at the community level.

Part 3

HOW TO SURVIVE —
AND
THRIVE

As Canada's first woman prime minister, Kim Campbell is among the small number of women in the world who have led a nation. The slow progress in the numbers of women leading a nation reflects the institutional and systemic barriers that challenge women inside and outside of political office.

It takes more than grit for women to end up in the winner's circle — and to stay there. A political journey rarely follows a straight line. Challenges and detours, including the media, money, and perceptions around age, will arise that will either push you to stay on course or sweep you off the road.

For some women, personal priorities such as health or family can overtake the importance of politics. The complex trade-offs that may ensue with a life in politics are sometimes judged not worth making. For other women, politics is their detour. Occasionally, women have been pushed from their path by the party or by the public, overtly or covertly. What does it take to stay the course? How do you decide if it's time to step back or change direction?

Holding a political office is a privilege that few get the chance to experience, but time in elected office eventually comes to an end. Whether your political popularity fades or your personal priorities shift, mobilizing the passion and energy that drove you into politics into a new direction is part of the journey.

Managing the Message

A free and independent press is paramount in a healthy democracy. Newsrooms and political journalists hold the "power of the pen" — *who* and *what* get reported on by the media shapes public knowledge and perception. Ultimately, the press has an obligation to deepen our understanding of the political landscape and women's place in it. But at all levels of politics, new media have changed our political conversations.

The advent of social media has empowered public figures to shape their own personal brand image and to grow a following online. Instagram, Facebook, YouTube, Twitter, and podcasting networks translate the traditional doorstep encounter into a digital space — but, as with traditional media, embracing social media and digital media has advantages and disadvantages. Libby Davies described social media as "both a powerful tool and a destructive weapon." Behind a cloak of anonymity online, the tenets of free speech are easily warped into hate speech. Nicole Sarauer, former leader of the Saskatchewan NDP, notes that online, people "say things … that they would never in a million years say to somebody's face."

In this section, women politicians discuss how they manage their public profile and their social media, while also containing and confronting misogyny. Among the women who share their experiences are Iqra Khalid, who put forward a motion to condemn racism and Islamophobia, M-103, Valérie Plante, whose campaign slogan, "the right man for the job," helped her unseat the Montreal mayor, and Sandra Jansen, who publicly addressed the violent, sexist comments being made about her by reading them aloud in the legislature.

IQRA KHALID

Iqra Khalid won a Liberal seat in Parliament in 2015 for Mississauga-Erin Mills. In 2016, Khalid introduced a non-binding motion to the House calling for the government of Canada to "condemn Islamophobia and all forms of systemic racism and religious discrimination." The motion passed in March 2017, prompting a tidal wave of both support and hatred on social media.

Canada is a multicultural country, and from our pluralism we have diverse values and perspectives. Together, we all contribute to a 360-degree outlook on issues and challenges. When I was preparing my motion, I wanted to include all types of systemic racism and religious discrimination. At that time, with so much hate and violence directed towards the Muslim community, I wanted to make sure that Islamophobia was not left out. This became Motion M-103, Systemic Racism and Religious Discrimination.

I tabled the motion in December 2016. It was voted on in March 2017 and passed by a majority vote with 201 in favour. The motion resulted in a study being conducted and the government dedicating $23 million to tackle the issues addressed in my motion.

I had just turned 30 years old, and my social media exploded. I was monitoring it personally and would read thousands of comments. Many of them were personal attacks, and there were numerous threats against my life.

I have Facebook, and I use it to talk to my residents from Mississauga-Erin Mills. I learned the power and the impact of social media in getting the message out and the importance of having the right message so that there's no room for misinterpretation. I have tens of thousands of followers on Facebook, and these are people who very regularly watch and follow whatever I'm doing. I am using it in a very positive way, and I encourage reasonable critical comments. At the same time, I make sure that obscenity and hate speech will not be tolerated.

That's what that forum is for: respectful discourse and not for hate speech. So, if there's one lesson I've learned, it is to monitor and to make sure that that is a free space for open ideas for everyone and to ignore the senseless haters. But the positive messages that are there, they keep me going.

66 *I make sure that obscenity and hate speech will not be tolerated.*

"

*I learned fairly
quickly about
the need to be
careful about the
way you phrase
your ideas when
you communicate
with the media.*

LYN MCLEOD

Lyn McLeod, a Liberal MPP from 1987 to 2003 and the leader of the Ontario Liberal Party from 1992 to 1996, describes the political power of the media and how easily a well-intentioned, thoughtful statement can be turned around to make an engaging, if not accurate, headline.

When I won and was appointed to cabinet, I went right away into my very first cabinet meeting and came out, not knowing about scrums, the media, and the 30-second sound bite. A reporter asked me what my goals were for colleges and universities. I said, "Well, I think I'll have to find out what colleges and universities feel they need before I set my goals." And the headline in the paper the next day was "New minister has no goals." So, I learned fairly quickly about the need to be careful about the way you phrase your ideas when you communicate with the media.

In another instance, the media asked me about my policy that when the court determines abuse has taken place, it is the abuser who should leave the house. When I was asked in a media scrum whether or not I would include verbal abuse in that, I said, "If the court determines that there is abuse, yes." The headline the next day was "Yell at your spouse, lose your house: McLeod."

"

*Anyone who
attacks my
policies is
welcome to
debate me.*

CANDICE BERGEN

Elected as the MP for Portage-Lisgar in Manitoba for the Conservative Party in 2008, 2011, and 2015, Candice Bergen was appointed Minister of State (Social Development) in 2013 and was Conservative House Leader in 2016. Throughout her political career, Bergen has been fielding personal attacks from the public.

Political figures have high public profiles. In politics, you assume the responsibility in the public sphere to use social media smartly. As a tool, it has great impact to help channel your brand and advance your party and its platform. Used smartly, it has impact. Anyone who attacks my policies is welcome to debate me. I totally respect that sparring of ideas and perspectives.

But personal attacks are off limits. I block nasty personal remarks and attempts to undermine my confidence. Give me a policy debate anytime. Attack me personally, and you have no space in my schedule or my mind. During the campaign, on E-day, we awoke to the fact that most of my lawn signs had been vandalized. Written on the signs across the riding was the word "Bimbo." People were mortified. I was not pleased. In the end, I think this illegal act served to mobilize, not diminish, my support. Like unnamed social media posts, people hide behind true debate and go nameless in these cowardly acts. Vandalizing is a sign of weakness. Give me open opportunity to debate, and I am ready with respect.

NIKI ASHTON

Niki Ashton used social media to announce her leadership bid for the federal NDP in 2017. She was pregnant at the time. Throughout her campaign, news headlines online read "NDP leadership hopeful Niki Ashton expecting twins" and "NDP leadership hopeful Niki Ashton says she's pregnant, continuing campaign."

This is not a case of freedom of speech; it is about hate.

The use of social media to stage announcements, hold online town halls, promote your brand, and engage constituents is powerful. In many respects — and for some — social media has almost entirely replaced traditional news sources. I used social media both as an MP and in my leadership bid as an effective two-way communication tool.

It has another side. Before the birth of my twins, I experienced ageism and sexism online. Messages arrived about being in political life while getting married and having children. How women and their partners manage family and public service is their personal decision and dynamic. Would young fathers have received the same questions about balancing family and politics? Neither should.

Social media provides a public stage where trolls can anonymously attack you. Women experience this disproportionately. Cowards can amplify their ignorance. This is not a case of freedom of speech; it is about hate. Privacy legislation by governments must be matched by proactive actions of social media company providers like Twitter and Facebook to prevent violent and vicious trolling. Canada's news channels also need policies to prevent the posting of unacceptable misogynist and sexist messages. More needs to be done on all three fronts: legislation, social media company actions, and newscast policy.

National leaders and public figures should never use misogynist language and divisive hate in overtones or undertones to drive their base and get their message out. It is unacceptable to cultivate society's lowest common denominator. As leaders, we have a moral responsibility to reflect the best qualities in our culture.

This is not about politics; it is about our common humanity.

JOANNE BERNARD

Joanne Bernard, a member of the Liberal Party, was elected to the Nova Scotia Legislature in 2013 representing Dartmouth North. As the first openly LGBTQ2+ person elected MLA in Nova Scotia, she spoke out against misogyny in politics.

Along with colleagues in Newfoundland and Alberta, I have been the target of cyberbullying. It is essential to take a strong and clear stand. Our young children are even more vulnerable. I will match any debate and criticism on policy. That's democracy. I am responsible to defend policy. But I will not tolerate bullying.

I am the first openly gay MLA in the history of Nova Scotia. My son was 23 at the time when he said, "Mom, I'm taking myself off social media. I can't bear to see you attacked and hurt." Homophobia started on the campaign trail and amplified when I was appointed to cabinet. Young girls and high school students see their leaders as targets of fat shaming, homophobia, and misogynist bullying. All women MLAs on all sides of the House are targets, and we carry a common challenge to confront bullying in all its forms. We made strides with an anti-harassment and cyberbullying law. Institutionally, within the bubble of government, things have lessened somewhat.

My advice to younger women is this: don't let these attacks and the experiences of elected women stop you. Reinforce your ability to step up and make a change. You can only do that by speaking out against bullying. I think that's why Cathy Bennett, myself, Carolyn Bennett, Sandra Jansen, Kathleen Quinn, Rachel Notley, all elected women across the country, are speaking up on the floor and putting remarks into the record. We are drawing the line in the sand. Television and newspapers must take the same unequivocal stand.

If you are not solving the problem, you are part of the problem. We need male colleagues and fathers and all high school teachers and students to stand up and speak out. Lives have been lost because of our silence. This is not about politics; it is about our common humanity.

SANDRA JANSEN

Sandra Jansen won a seat in the Alberta Legislature for the PC Party in 2012. While running in the Alberta PC leadership race in 2016, Jansen received abuse and harassment and ultimately withdrew from the campaign. A short time later, she crossed the floor to join the NDP.

Why should anyone "put up with" degradation?

I spent a long time as a journalist — 23 years. When I moved back to Calgary in 2007, I was wrapping up my journalism career to go back to school and get my master's. I continued to work in television because I was lucky enough to get an anchor position on a show to work around my schoolwork. Journalism gives you a special skill zeroing in on issues. It also affords you a platform to highlight issues.

In my leadership bid, I put on social media some of the things being said about me. It did not get a lot of traction with colleagues or retraction by the authors. When I crossed the floor, things escalated even more. Trying to deal with these attacks alone was not stopping anything. It was only when I stood up in the legislature and read the comments into the official record that an uproar was created.

It happens to a lot of women and girls who bear the brunt of violence alone. You can feel the pressure to ignore it. Comments to "put up with it, that's just what happens to women in public life" —

that's not good enough. Why does this happen? Why should anyone "put up with" degradation?

I read aloud comments including posts that I should wear a bulletproof pantsuit. The legislature listened as I read into the records comments by shameful, nameless trolls. The response was immediate by women across the country on school boards, city councils, in legislatures, and in Parliament. Comments poured in from women telling me about their own experience. Bringing this hate into the sunlight had opened a floodgate. Silent no more, women and men must legislate where possible, work with media companies when possible, and directly promote the protection of girls and women against online hate happening in our society. Staying silent is just not an option for me.

INDIRA NAIDOO-HARRIS

We cannot be a bystander when someone is being bullied.

Indira Naidoo-Harris was a member of the Legislative Assembly of Ontario for the Ontario Liberal Party from 2014 to 2018, representing the riding of Halton and served in various cabinet positions, including Minister of the Status of Women. Her entry into politics came alongside personal attacks.

No one can sit on the sidelines if there is an ugly tweet or something posted on Facebook that is hateful. Everybody is part of a larger community and larger world, both online and in our communities. It takes an entire village to build a civil society.

I am a woman of colour and an immigrant to Canada. My family gave me a strong foundation to face adversity. We lived under apartheid. My family taught me this: bullying is not my shame but the shame of the perpetrator. Someone yelling a racial slur as I walk down a street speaks volumes about the person who does not have the courage of conviction to speak to me personally and rationally.

We cannot be a bystander when someone is being bullied. We must approach it head-on. I taught my kids to act — I did it myself. If I saw something happening that made me uncomfortable, I needed to act. By being a bystander, you are allowing bullying to occur and creating a culture of acceptance of hatred. That is not okay. Each of us needs to expose bullying for what it is — a cowardly act. Each adversity I have faced made me stronger. Facing down hate and bullying has built my character. We are a stronger society when we all understand that this is a global family we are building. Alone we will accomplish nothing in comparison to what we can accomplish together. Alone we are just one person. Together we stand on the shoulders of everyone around us. We move forward one conversation at a time.

JENNY KWAN

Jenny Kwan served as a Vancouver city councillor from 1993 to 1996 and was elected as the MLA for Vancouver-Mount Pleasant in 1996 for the NDP, becoming one of the first Chinese Canadians to sit in the Legislative Assembly. Re-elected as an MLA in 2001, 2005, 2009, and 2013 and elected as an MP in 2015 for Vancouver East for the NDP, Kwan, like many other women in this book, has found herself under fire on social media.

Hate mail came to me anonymously through social media, letters, and voicemails. Whatever the format, it can be extremely hurtful and it does get to you. So, here is my hard-earned advice to other women: You need to put into place a buffer. You need to take care of yourself. We're all human, and it does impact you. In those moments, when you need to self-preserve, to recharge, here is what I suggest: surround yourself with people you can lean on and trust. Find someone with whom you can talk. Let someone take care of you. Find your comfort. For me, that meant my mom would bring me her chicken soup.

> *Surround yourself with people you can lean on and trust.*

JEAN AUGUSTINE

Jean Augustine was the first Black woman to be elected to the House of Commons in 1993 and the first Black woman to be appointed to cabinet. While in office, Augustine, a Liberal MP, helped establish February as Black History Month nationwide.

A little advice? Make the decision: get engaged. Work with the media so that they "see" your character and policies, not your clothes. Include men as pivotal mentors and supporters. And — know that you will have to work, as a Black woman, twice as hard to show your merit. Fortunately, you will be able to do that. You are already outstanding.

The contributions of Black women are often invisible. With the Vice-President of Equity and Community Inclusion of Ryerson University, Dr. Denise O'Neil Green, Dauna Jones-Simmonds and I have been working to render visible remarkable Black women in Canada. The book *100 Accomplished Black Canadian Women* (100ABC Women), both 2016 and 2018 versions, celebrates 100 Black women leaders. We are now working on 2020.

AUDREY MCLAUGHLIN

Elected to the House of Commons in 1987 for the NDP, Audrey McLaughlin was the first woman chair of the parliamentary caucus of a federal party. In 1989, McLaughlin became the first woman to lead a national political party and served as leader of the federal NDP in Parliament until 1997.

I remember once that the media reported two women had worn the same jacket to Parliament. It struck me as absurd. There were some 250 men who were in the same suit. I do not mean to make light. Internationally, some women risk their lives to stand for elected office. That's worth reporting.

When I first entered Parliament, a media person said, "I suppose you will only focus on women's issues?" I replied, "Yes, absolutely. I will be working on the economy, the environment, housing, poverty, daycare, and human rights." So, there is this thing about women taking power. Sharing power, promoting societal policies, and, yes, protecting girls and women and addressing discrimination are a part of it all. On some issues, you must time your intervention. You are not retreating, just timing. Sometimes, you have to say to yourself, I will fight that battle, absolutely, just not now.

MORGANE OGER

Morgane Oger entered politics as the NDP candidate for the Vancouver-False Creek riding in the 2017 BC provincial election. Determined to help redefine the political landscape, Oger sought to leverage her presence on social media as an advocate for social justice but was defeated by 1.7 percent of the vote.

As a trans woman, I had survived many attacks and was still standing.

When I entered politics, I already had a huge following on social media as a social justice activist. I was already tested and credible. By the time the party vetted me, I had gone through so many hurdles. The road to the nomination is a big test. I already had some 12 000 tweets under my belt in managing social media. As a trans woman, I had survived many attacks and was still standing. Know social media. Develop strong networks. Understand the path ahead very clearly.

My advice to women, especially intersectional women with added challenges of race, ethnicity, and sexual orientation, is to get active in social media well ahead of entering politics. Organize your networks of support. I was active with school boards, parent-teacher associations, and professional networks. I cultivated a solid presence on LinkedIn. Leverage your support groups ahead of entering politics. It is already very difficult to enter politics as a trans woman. Be prepared.

Build your story. My narrative had to be clear and strong. There are two levels to the game. One level is the personal narrative. The other level is the ground game. The ground game needs people who believe in you. Have no illusions. You need a team that believes in you, in your nomination, and in your race.

I had to learn the boundaries of the press and how to manage them. I needed to know how to keep the wolves at bay about things that are important to me and protect my family. One of my boundaries was my children. My children had already been threatened. I had already dealt with the fear that someone would harm them to hurt me. I sought and received pragmatic advice. Don't forget that the press has a vested interest in you speaking to them. If they burn you, they burn their own bridges. We had to develop mutual respect and appropriate boundaries. They have children and families too. We sat down and outlined mutual boundaries, and both respected the guidelines.

KATHLEEN WYNNE

Kathleen Wynne, the first woman premier and the first openly gay premier in Canada (2013–2018), was subject to misogynistic and sexist attacks while Liberal premier of Ontario. Wynne believes that legislators need to protect the most vulnerable from these attacks.

Dealing with the whiplash of social media is a huge societal question for all of us to struggle with. Our society needs to work together to build civility and common cause.

We have brought in policy changes to support women who are discriminated against. The question on social media is an important one. The violence — and quite frankly the hate and division — has been stirred up by the US presidential election. Large wounds have been opened and reopened recklessly.

Just imagine young girls and vulnerable women trying to deal with pervasive negativity. I am more concerned with our children, and particularly girls, and how they are taught how to manage online media. Legislators need to make clear progress to protect the vulnerable.

Our society needs to work together to build civility and common cause.

RANA BOKHARI

When Rana Bokhari was leader of the Manitoba Liberal Party and was subject to harassment online, she received support from colleagues across all party lines.

Many of the older generation are not high users of social media. They pick up the paper and make their ballot box decisions based on all-candidates debates and traditional news sources like the *Winnipeg Sun* and the *Winnipeg Free Press*. Papers have the responsibility to promote free speech but also to protect citizens against hate speech.

Online, we hired a social media company to help use social media for maximum impact. When the attacks started happening, with racist and sexist comments, it was time to speak out. I was amazed and grateful for cross-party support. Women across political lines are all allies in confronting baseless, nameless misogyny. Nahanni Fontaine, an Indigenous woman and amazing NDP MLA in Manitoba, and Rochelle Squires, the PC Minister responsible for Status of Women, were both admirable in defending me when vicious, racist remarks circulated in 2016.

There is nothing partisan about misogyny. It is baseless and hits women and girls across the board. Adding race and ethnicity only heightens the need for public figures to stand up against all attacks. It is all the stronger when men are just as bold to confront misogyny and promote a strong, caring, inclusive society.

"

There is nothing partisan about misogyny.

VALÉRIE PLANTE

When Valérie Plante, then city councillor and leader of Projet Montréal, entered the 2017 municipal election for mayor of Montreal, she trailed the well-known incumbent by a large margin.

Communication was central to our campaign. Open, engaging, clear, and aggressive, we went straight to the people. I rode my bicycle, took buses, walked streets, and spoke with everyone I could. We offered a progressive, coherent, and purposeful vision. Getting our message out and widely broadcast was central to our success. I am a graduate of anthropology, museology, and multiethnic intervention and am convinced of the power of smart media. But when the team unveiled the suggested slogan for the campaign, I had to catch my breath. I am a feminist. I believe fundamentally in diversity and inclusivity. Our party is committed to these principles in appointments to executive committee and city structures where possible.

So, when the slogan was suggested, it made me think twice. "L'homme de la situation" is a common French phrase meaning "the right man for the job." In the end, I convinced myself. It was a catchy play on words, even a bit irreverent. Still, I didn't sleep much that night wondering what my feminist friends would think as we sprang out of the starting blocks with our energy-packed campaign and its slogan the next morning. We had an immediate 20 requests for media interviews.

I had to leave behind the part of me hoping to be "loved by all" when I ran for leadership and mayor. You must fight for certain causes, and that will not always translate into everyone liking you. Projet Montréal ran as a team. The odds were against us, so we had to be bold, audacious, and certainly not boring.

We were running against a giant. Yes, we encountered social media attacks along the path of politics. Social media can be harsh. Unnamed people can hide behind a screen. Since I have been elected, I have known two cases that went to trial. You must confront violence and involve the police when needed.

In the end, we prevailed. We had a small, talented, and highly focused communication team at the core of our campaign. It all came together at the doors, on the buses, in bike lanes, and with smart media at the heart of the campaign.

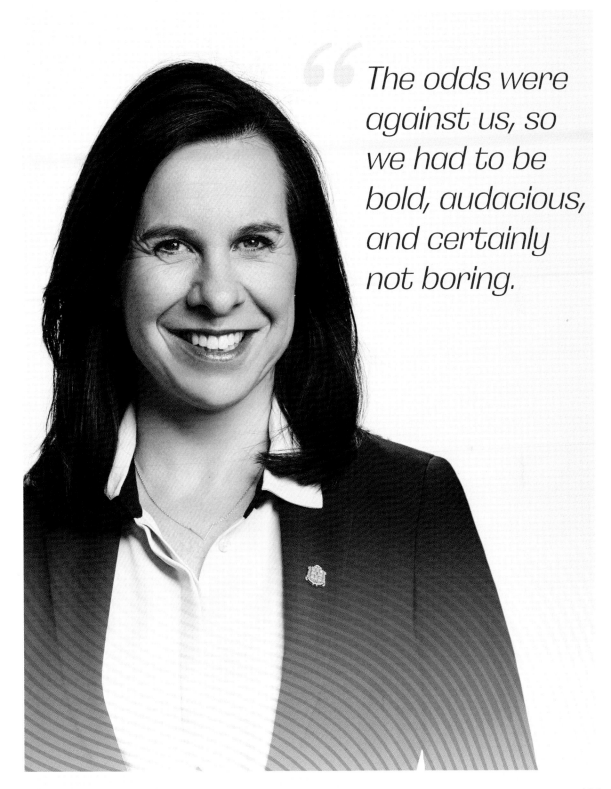

> *The odds were against us, so we had to be bold, audacious, and certainly not boring.*

> *Cyberbullying legislation had just been passed in Nova Scotia, and the police advised me to report the sexual harassment.*

LENORE ZANN

Lenore Zann was elected to the Nova Scotia Legislature in 2009, 2013, and 2017 for the NDP. Before becoming involved in politics, Zann was an actor who had worked in film, on TV and radio, and in theatre. Her career as an actor opened her up to social media attacks that she had to learn how to manage.

At the age of 19, I landed the starring role of Marilyn Monroe in a rock opera, *Hey Marilyn!* In 2004, I wrote my own play *The Marilyn Tapes*, which I performed Off-Broadway, once more playing Marilyn Monroe. Some scenes in my career involved nudity. When I entered politics, I discussed this with the NDP.

Back then, I was new to Twitter. After an event one night, I saw someone had tweeted a picture of me topless, a freeze-frame from a scene in the popular TV series *The L Word*. The comment with it was "Where's the old Lenore now?" I didn't know who or where this person was. I wrote back, "Well the new Lenore is kicking butt in the Nova Scotia Legislature. Please delete this photo." Then I went to bed.

The next day, a torrent of tweets had arrived with all kinds of lewd comments. This was 2013. I was naive about this media platform. My sister, a teacher, urged me to report the tweets to the police. Cyberbullying legislation had just been passed in Nova Scotia, and the police advised me to report the sexual harassment, so I started the process.

The media got hold of the story, and the next thing I knew, a "Freedom of Speech" lawyer was claiming that I had no right to ask the young man to delete the topless freeze-frame from *The L Word* because the image was public (not addressing the fact that it was a stolen image from a TV series with a copyright). The lawyer wrote an op-ed in our local paper with the headline "Who's the real bully?"

It was a horrendous experience being piled on like that — attacked, shamed, and humiliated publicly. And I had no one to turn to. Nobody in government came to my aid or even offered any sympathy — not even in my own small NDP caucus — nobody except the cybersquad folks who had helped shut down the original perpetrator. I learned a lot about politicians from this experience.

Finding the Money

There's no way around it: campaigns cost money. Raising it, spending it, and reporting it are all tightly controlled by election laws based on the Canada Elections Act. The cost of campaign headquarters, lawn signs, insurance for offices and campaign liabilities, phones, computers, and advertising — everything adds up. While the strict limit set on how much candidates can contribute to their own campaign is intended to level the playing field and prevent wealthy individuals from having an advantage, for some, the cost can be the determining barrier to entry. For candidates whose financial realities include loan payments, daycare, and more, the cost of running for office can be prohibitive.

While pay equity is protected under the Canadian Human Rights Act, the wage gap, along with the overall devaluation of women's work, persists in Canada. According to Statistics Canada data, full-time working white women are paid 75 cents for every dollar earned by men in Canada. This gap widens for women of colour, for Indigenous women, for women living with a disability, and for newcomers to Canada. With this wage gap, it is clear that the financial costs of a campaign may deter many women from participating. Attracting a diverse range of women to politics needs thoughtful strategies and solid financial support.

Leadership campaign limits are set by political parties, while the total spending limits for federal campaign candidates are set by Elections Canada and are based on the number of electors at the time of the election. While the expenses are similar for all candidates, personal earning power and access to networks of financial support differ, and women, traditionally, are disadvantaged. The stories in this section help you learn how to "find the money."

> **I had to learn quickly that asking for help was a strength and a necessity.**

CAROLINE COCHRANE

Caroline Cochrane, who is of Métis descent, was elected to the Legislative Assembly of the Northwest Territories in 2015, representing Range Lake. Cochrane has served in a number of cabinet positions, most recently as Minister of Education, Culture and Employment and Minister Responsible for the Status of Women.

I never had any money or mentors, and I never really knew what I was doing. But I had a few great women friends and my wonderful family, who stood by me through the political campaign.

Life was never easy, but I was never known to turn away from a challenge. Becoming a single mom made me realize I needed to change my own life, so I returned to school and got a degree in social work. I spent over 20 years working with low-income families and homeless women, and I struggled to understand why the government never provided adequate support when the need was so evident. I wanted change; we needed change! People always told me, "You can change from the inside or the outside." They were right. But one day, I realized the most potential for change was from the top. That's the day I decided to run for MLA.

As women, we have been socialized to be humble, and I've always been fiercely independent, so to ask for any help was a huge barrier for me. I had to learn quickly that asking for help was a strength and a necessity. Most importantly, for fundraising, I had to learn to ask for money. I had been used to doing that for housing and poverty in our community. But that was always raising money for others. Asking for money for myself, for my own campaign, seemed so different and difficult. I was so surprised when the first person I asked said, "I want to give you money." It was such a boost to my confidence. I had to learn to ask for my own needs. That was new.

Campaigning can be tough, but whenever I felt like giving up, I thought of those depending on me to make things better and the amazing people supporting me. This kept me going. Winning the election and then becoming a minister was an incredible honour. I'm hopeful that other Métis women, single mothers, women in poverty, and women working in the non-profit sector will see in me that chance to make it in politics. I hope my success will open the path for them.

Political victory may only last a short time, but with a lot of hard work, you can make a lot of positive change.

KIM ZIPPEL

Kim Zippel ran unsuccessfully for city councillor in Peterborough in 2014; she ran again and was elected councillor for Otonabee Ward 1 in 2018. Her budget was tight, but she was determined to use the money that she had efficiently and keep within the budget she set.

We set a clear budget, below the permitted elections limits and within our reach.

The first time I ran for city council was a huge learning curve for me. As someone new to politics, I wasn't comfortable asking for money for myself. I didn't even have a donate button on my website.

I was hoping to sell my ideas and platform at the door. I had to learn to be very clear about what I needed. Learning how to sell yourself, your ideas, ask for people's vote, then ask for money — in the space of a door knock — was foreign to me. I am trained in science. I know what precision means. But those skills didn't translate over to politics. It takes time to build relationships with volunteers and the voters; it's more interpersonal. But you don't have that kind of time at the door, so as a first-time candidate, it was very difficult for me when it came time to ask for support for the campaign, especially financial.

In my first bid for city council, my husband and I wanted to limit our financial risk. We had a small, tight team. We needed to use everyone's energy very wisely. We set a clear budget, below the permitted elections limits and within our reach. I learned a great deal about campaign financing. We researched sustainable practices and energy-saving techniques. With realistic goals and clear financial boundaries, we tapped into all cost-saving ways of communicating by press interviews, website, social media, and sheer footwork going door to door.

I came to realize the importance of many small donations. They show you how broad your support is across the community. I didn't budget for electronic signs flashing at busy intersections, expensive paid ads, and glossy brochures. I hand-delivered my platform to many. In an older community, not always on computers, that was appreciated.

In the end, we successfully came in on budget, and while I did not succeed against the two incumbents, I learned a great deal. Our campaign gave our team solid fiscal discipline and left me in a strong position to pick up the pieces and walk away with lessons learned and the determination to run again.

I would think that raising money after a campaign loss is very difficult. Your momentum swiftly disappears. Setting realistic expectations enabled us to complete all of our campaign financial and legal obligations in a strong position at the end of it all, and we didn't need to seek or accept post-voting day donations.

Men have deeper pockets than most women.

ALEXA MCDONOUGH

In 1980, Alexa McDonough was elected to lead the Nova Scotia NDP, the first woman to lead a provincial party in the province. McDonough served in the provincial legislature from 1981 until she won leadership of the federal NDP in 1995, succeeding Audrey McLaughlin. McDonough was elected as an MP for Halifax in 1997, served as leader until 2002, and retired from politics in 2008.

There's no question that there was a big affirmative action movement within the NDP. Some barriers for women are financial. We were always raising money for the "Women in Legislature" (WIL) fund provincially and the "Participation of Women"

(POW) federally. We were constantly raising money to mount small themed workshops to help women build their confidence and build their skills. Men have deeper pockets than most women, especially NDP women, with our deep connection to labour and unions. The NDP has been relentless in trying to find ways to help women overcome financial barriers.

Politics is a team sport. No one does it alone. You must be pretty egocentric to claim you made something happen yourself. We are very intentional in our support for women in leadership.

DIANE THERRIEN

In 2014, at the age of 28, Diane Therrien ran for city council and won. Four years later, when she declared her intention to unseat the mayor, people were energized. Therrien was elected mayor of Peterborough in 2018 at the age of 32 with close to 70 percent of the vote.

We wanted to be concrete and creative in how we asked for financial support.

During a campaign, especially if change is in the air, people appreciate your stance to take on an entrenched incumbent. I advanced a progressive, fresh vision for the city. People got excited about the campaign and were willing to invest. Even before we put out the call for funding, people were asking how they could help.

We wanted to be concrete and creative in how we asked for financial support. We linked donations to specific outcomes: this amount would buy so many signs; this amount would buy a radio ad. We wanted each person who invested money in the campaign to feel the value of their investment. We wanted to make it tangible to them and to send out an immediate thank you the moment we received a donation.

Especially at the tail end of the campaign, when we needed to ramp up our visibility and scale up our efforts as we crossed the finish line, all donations — from $2 to $200 — counted as a strong final get-out-the-vote push.

RANA BOKHARI

Rana Bokhari ran for Liberal Party leadership in Manitoba in 2013. While the entry fee varies by party and level of government, for Bokhari, it involved either a sum or money or a set level of membership sales.

The leadership package required candidates to either pay $1,500 or bring in a certain number of memberships. I had just graduated from law school and received my call to the bar and was beginning a career. It was a lot of money for me to even enter the race. The only way I was going to be able to pay the entry fee and mount a campaign was to attract large numbers of new people to the party. The old established Liberals were not my natural voters. I needed to seek out and recruit new members across the province. At $10 a membership, we reached out widely and sold between 800 and 1000 memberships. After winning the leadership, I was paid about $1,600 per month for three years while trying to build the party toward the next election. It was very expensive.

It was a lot of money for me to even enter the race.

Age Is Overrated

Attracting Canadians with a range of ages to run for political office is vital — after all, decisions about public policy often have a significant impact on generations of Canadians and are made by a select few. But while there is a real "can-do" determination among women of all ages to participate in politics, a "can't-do" attitude confronts many women at both ends of the spectrum: women who want to become involved in politics are sometimes seen as either too young or too old. Yet these debates about age have not stopped the women in this book — RoseAnne Archibald was just 23 years old when she first became Chief, and Hazel McCallion was 93 years old when she retired as mayor of Mississauga.

LIBBY DAVIES

Libby Davies served on Vancouver City Council from 1982 to 1993 and as an MP for Vancouver East for the NDP from 1997 to 2015. She retired from Parliament before the 2015 federal election after 18 years as an MP.

Age and politics absolutely depend on the person.

Age and politics absolutely depend on the person. I always ask myself, Do you have the stamina? I work very, very hard. I love doing politics, but it takes stamina. It is not a case of numerical age. Turning 65 was not the issue.

The issue for me was always the willingness and capacity to tackle the work with enthusiasm. It takes a lot of physical energy to be always on the front line and in the public eye. That's a big and a personal decision. It's stamina and personal commitment that count. Ageism is a false hurdle.

HEDY FRY

Hedy Fry, a member of the Liberal Party, is the longest-serving woman MP in Canadian history. She has won every election since her first in 1993. She sees age as only one of the barriers that women may face.

I t was hard to understand that some people in politics view age as a drawback. Your accumulated experience is no longer something of paramount importance to decision-making. Age seems to overshadow acquired professionalism as a valued asset.

The hardest thing for me as a woman in politics, coming out of medicine, was to adjust to the reality that a lot in politics depends on your geographic district and factors other than merit or experience. Everything I had achieved in life before politics was fuelled by my technical training and capability.

I do understand regionalism in terms of representing issues from regional perspectives. And intersectionality is paramount in terms of promoting missing voices. Age is an overrated and unnecessary barrier.

Age is an overrated and unnecessary barrier.

ROSEMARY GANLEY

Rosemary Ganley was a municipal candidate when she was in her early seventies and was appointed to Prime Minister Justin Trudeau's G7 Gender Equality Advisory Council when she was in her eighties. She believes that people of all ages have a place in Canadian politics.

I think there is ageism in Canadian culture. Perhaps it is less in Indigenous communities, where Elders are highly regarded. Being set aside as too old to have an impact or make a contribution is very wasteful to our society. I'd like to challenge ageism. A new paradigm of using human talent, no matter what the age, is important to our society. We're not there yet. Older, seasoned people are often set aside. I said to my doctor, "I'm nearly 80." He replied, "Rosemary, I've got five patients that are 100. So, let's just leave that open." Sometimes you don't know how old you are until you look in the mirror.

> " *I would never rule out seeking political office at any age or at any stage of life.*

I think that's why I would like older women in office. They have come to valuable conclusions. I'd like those insights to be at the decision-making table in public policy. They should be at the tables where basic income is discussed. There would not be so many homeless if we moved to a basic income in Canada.

Men's experience is different. Age is seen as career-building. For women, age is seen as a reason to sideline. I reject the premise. I would never rule out seeking political office at any age or at any stage of life. We are all valuable.

PHYLLIS WILLIAMS

Elders are a deep well of wisdom and steady guidance for younger generations in Indigenous communities as described by Phyllis Williams, Chief of Curve Lake First Nation since 2012.

In 2019, Curve Lake First Nation community released a booklet and CD summarizing a set of interviews and dialogue sessions conducted by the youth of our community with Elders. In a remarkable experience, bringing together Trent University videography students, the Peterborough Rotary Club, and Curve Lake representatives, our Elders shared their wisdom and stories of how the culture of a community and its language provide a strong bond to help all members through the rough periods and life-altering changes. The younger children at the Curve Lake First Nation School drew colourful pictures for the booklet. The CD and booklet are in both Ojibwe and English. This project, called the "Seeds of Good Life," celebrates the significance of Elders, the language and knowledge keepers, in guiding us and the legacy of youth in protecting culture and language. Above all, Elders shared their life experiences in helping the community to continue to be resilient. We hold a deep respect for our Elders with the relationship they have with leadership and the youth of the community.

> *We hold a deep respect for our Elders.*

Complex Trade-Offs

Can women have it all? Can anyone? Niki Ashton was pregnant when she ran for the leadership of the NDP in 2017; she joined one leadership candidate debate by conference call when her due date precluded her from flying. A few years earlier, newly elected federal member Sana Hassainia, in order not to miss a vote, had to take her infant into the House since there was no parental leave for MPs (and there still isn't). In 2018, federal member Karina Gould captured media attention when she breastfed her baby in the House. She tweeted, "No shame in breastfeeding! Baby's gotta eat & I had votes. Clearly still work to do … Glad @HoCSpeaker & parl colleagues supportive! :)"

Everyone — including aspiring politicians — must juggle the time, energy, and focus required to hold a job, nurture a family, maintain friendships, and for some, raise children and sometimes provide caregiving for other family members. Striving to be meaningfully present on all fronts, let alone take time for self-care, stretches anyone's capabilities. Meanwhile the nature of work, including shift work, short-term contracts, and unpaid domestic labour, can be a roadblock to women's entry into politics. The question "Can women have it all?" is really asking "Do women have the same choices as men?" In a culture that relies on women to be disproportionately responsible for domestic labour and child-rearing, the answer is often clear.

And as women candidates continue to receive gendered public criticism, the media glare and the online attacks also have an impact on the candidate's family. While candidates are coached on how to navigate personal attacks, their families must also learn to manage the public criticism. There is no time out in politics. Going to the supermarket, the bank, shopping, concerts, or places of worship all become public events. Choosing to run for office may involve complex personal trade-offs. Many women, in weighing the trade-offs, involved their families in their political pursuit and described the unique and sometimes surprising ways that their families supported them.

LYN MCLEOD

Lyn McLeod was first elected as a Liberal MPP in 1987. In 1992, she became the first woman to lead a major political party in Ontario. Before beginning her career in politics, McLeod and her family estimated what this time commitment would entail, particularly the impact on their family life.

We spent the next day as a family talking about what [winning] would mean.

I had never intended to enter politics. I spent 16 years on the school board, five years as chair, and was locally active at the community level. It was an era before teachers had the right to strike. There were some issues which provoked a walkout. It caused a great deal of soul-searching. We needed to address a significant change in administration and brought in somebody focused on building relationships and conflict resolution. So, my key learnings were around public management of issues and conflict resolution management. All were important skills for politics later.

Was saying yes to politics easy? I had gone back to school as a mature student, completed my master's degree in psychology, and was working in a hospital setting with children and youth. I was absolutely committed to my work, so when the party asked me to run politically, my instinct was to say, "No, this is not the route I want to go." I also had four daughters; two of my daughters were away in university, two were still at home.

I did the analysis. The party was likely to win the next election, and the potential to impact policy was compelling. We spent the next day as a family talking about what it would mean. I was somewhat naïve. I sat down with a former member and asked, "What does this mean in terms of time?" And he said, "Well, the legislature sits about 17 weeks a year." So, as a family, we thought, "Okay. We could probably manage 17 weeks a year," recognizing that provincial politics coming from Thunder Bay meant that I was going to be away all week. My younger daughter, who was just in Grade 8, said, "Oh, Mom, I don't know if I could manage if you were away that much." And the daughter who was two years older said, "Kristen, don't worry, by the time Mom gets elected, you'll be in high school. That won't matter." The reality of the time commitment would hit much later!

LISA RAITT

Before being elected as an MP for the Conservative Party in 2008 for Halton, Ontario — later Milton — Lisa Raitt was president and CEO of the Toronto Port Authority. Raitt believes that the decision to leave business and enter politics can curtail the possibility of successfully returning to the private sector on the same career track.

I can only speak to my own experience, but once you reach a certain level in the corporate world and you see promotion or you see promise, it's really hard to exit business and enter politics.

Your motivation has to be crystal clear. Many may think, "Oh, I will just go back." In my view, that may not be the case. It's really difficult to go back once you've left and become partisan — especially if you have taken very controversial stances. Furthermore, consider appointments. If you think of going the diplomat route, it may be very difficult depending on the government in power. So, in a lot of ways, politics is a one-way street from the corporate world. You have to ask, "Why would I take that risk?" Most women in the corporate world have salaries that will not be matched in politics, and you have to calculate university for the kids, care for sick family members, mortgages, and retirement into the decision-making process too. Politics is only for a short period of time. It's a big calculus for a woman in business.

You have to ask, "Why would I take that risk?"

KELLY REGAN

Kelly Regan's husband, Geoff, was elected to the House of Commons in 1993 as the MP for Halifax West and was in office when she ran for the Nova Scotia Legislature for Bedford-Birch Cove in 2009. She was elected as an MLA for the Liberal Party in 2009 and re-elected in 2013 and 2017.

How do you figure out how to have two parents in demanding posts in politics and still juggle everything? It wasn't always easy. The day of my swearing-in was the day of my son's graduation. I was devastated when I found out there was a conflict and went to break the news to my son that I couldn't attend his graduation. "Oh, Mom," he replied. "I'm not going to that. I'm coming with you." The whole family came to the swearing-in, and then they bolted to his graduation. It was Grade 6, but I felt that first absence deeply.

With two of us in politics, whoever is not in the middle of an election is the PIC — parent in charge. We use cellphones to stay in touch constantly. Because my son was in junior high, he would text me every day to let me know he was home after school. I could step out of the House so that we could talk. It's demanding, but lots of families deal with this. We all stayed connected and supported each other.

In the beginning, I didn't do early morning breakfast meetings or fundraisers. I wanted that time with our son — his sisters were off at university, and his dad was usually in Ottawa. Back then, it was family time. But that didn't prevent other people from commenting on our family situation. A lovely older gentleman at church expressed concern about my son — how was he making do without me around as much? I told him, "Oh, you don't have to worry. His grades have gone up since I got elected."

Being present for the family was easier for me in provincial politics than Geoff in federal politics. I could be home every night. But it takes a lot of organization to do the work you love, serving your constituents in the legislature and being with the people you love at home.

KAREN MCCRIMMON

Karen McCrimmon has been an MP for the Liberal Party for Kanata-Carleton in Ontario since 2015. McCrimmon was appointed parliamentary secretary to the Minister of Public Safety and Emergency Preparedness in 2018.

The best things in life aren't easy. Love isn't easy, kids aren't easy, spouses aren't easy, and neither is politics. So, my message to women would be "You've got to be strong." I don't mind a little bit of struggle. That's earning your stripes. Politics will not be given to you on a platter. Politics is demanding. But the best things in life are.

Women have a hard time saying no. Any week on the Hill, I may receive over 100 invitations. At first, I tried doing it all. I talked to some male MPs, and they offered this advice: "I look after my health, my nutrition, my sleep, and my life first." Yet many of the women I talked to were not doing that. Like me, they were trying to do it all. If you're not healthy, you can't perform.

Parliamentary schedules are demanding. We need to use instruments like gender analysis to maximum impact in a consistent way across the board. In doing so, we need to be clear about what we want to achieve and which instruments will get us to that result. Nothing is straightforward. Nothing is easy, and it's often not the direct levers that get us to where we want to go. We need to ask, "Who has control? Who can influence this?" A lot of the work done in Parliament is actually done through indirect influence.

The best things in life aren't easy ... and neither is politics.

ROCHELLE SQUIRES

Rochelle Squires, elected to the Legislative Assembly of Manitoba for the PC Party in 2016 in the riding of Riel, stresses the importance of maintaining healthy relationships as a politician. Squires serves as Minister of Sustainable Development and Minister responsible for Francophone Affairs and Status of Women.

My children are older. We stay in touch by text. My mother lives in another province. She watches Question Period every day and keeps her friends posted on my performance. She also texts me her thoughts. I set date nights with my husband and each of my children. I need to be sure, first and foremost, the family front is steady. Relationships break down if they are ignored, I know. And I know how incredibly difficult it is when the home front is destabilized. It's debilitating for everyone. There's a lot of stress and time demands in politics. Home is a safe haven.

The staff is also a team and a family of a kind. Along with the family of fellow members of the legislature, they all provide another safety net.

KIM ZIPPEL

In 2018, Kim Zippel was elected to city council and spoke about the toll that running can take on a family, both in time and money. Since a position on city council is often considered part-time, as is the remuneration, the fear is that only people who can afford the job will be able to run.

I didn't make it to many of my family events, so people just set a place card for me at the table. You are on the go all the time. There's a lack of sleep. There's financial and physical stress. You really need the understanding of all the family.

I was so very lucky in this manner. My husband was core to the campaign too — organizing daily canvassing routes, delivering signs, and cooking meals. When I say, "The first thing I did after signing the papers to enter the race was to phone supporters," by that I meant, I phoned my family. I first discussed the decision with my husband and then called my son and my father. The decision was made as a family. I had their full support.

Paying for the cost of running is not very family-friendly for many. And if you are elected, the lower salaries on municipal councils can be problematic for people with families. It might be eliminating a whole slice of very talented people in the community who just can't afford to undertake the serious workload of council if they are not financially solid enough to carry all the costs. Council is a considerable time commitment with a limited salary, a reality to consider for all candidates.

BONNIE CROMBIE

Bonnie Crombie became the MP for Mississauga-Streetsville in Ontario for the Liberal Party in 2008. In 2011, after losing her seat, she transitioned successfully to municipal politics and won a seat on the Mississauga City Council in a by-election. In 2014, after Hazel McCallion retired, Crombie entered the mayoral race, won, and was re-elected in 2018.

Family considerations may influence your decision of when and at what level to get into politics.

I t takes a lot of planning and thought to bridge being a young parent and a parliamentarian. It can be an important factor in choosing the level of electoral politics to pursue. Running municipally, or in some cases, provincially instead of federally, may mean you don't have to either leave your family while the legislature is sitting or transplant the family to the capital city. I waited until my children were a lot older until I decided to run. Family considerations may influence your decision of when and at what level to get into politics.

> *Don't try to imagine yourself being a mom half the day and a candidate half the day. Be a mom and a candidate full-time.*

ELIZABETH MAY

Elizabeth May, leader of the Green Party of Canada, invites her party's candidates to involve their families on the campaign trail. Creating family-friendly campaign rooms including access to changing tables, toys, and babysitters, is essential to building inclusive campaign teams.

I say to women who are thinking of running: "Don't try to imagine yourself being a mom half the day and a candidate half the day. Be a mom and a candidate full-time." Some of the Green Party candidates had small babies and children. I made them feel welcome to invite children to be involved. Canvassing can be fun [for children] — it's outdoors, and you're with your mom. Slightly older children often get quite involved volunteering decorating headquarters and banging in lawn signs. We need to break down barriers so that women feel comfortable being both parent and candidate.

When I was on a contract with Sierra Club, I didn't qualify for maternity leave. I was either going to bring my daughter to work or work from home. The Sierra Club had a baby-in-the-office policy, with encouraged baby-zones. I have never had what you would call work-life balance. I never thought of it as carving out time away from work to be with my kids. My kids are my life, and my work is my life. I just bring the two together. You do have to be so careful. Weekends can get chewed up with political events. So, I tell women, "Carve out play time for you. And to the best of your ability, guard both your family and the issues that drive your life."

Women always ask me what politics will mean for their family. They want to know what the impact will be and how parties and politicians manage it. Women also invariably ask me [when I ask them to run], "Are you sure you can't find someone better?" It must be socialization. Men might say, "I've got a lot on my plate. I have to think about whether I can make room right now. I've considered it and believe I would be a great MP, but I'm not sure the time is right now." Women with so many accomplishments ask if I can't find someone better. It takes a lot of persuasion and many phone calls. Those phone calls always involve concerns about family finances and the stability of the family.

CATHERINE MCKENNA

Elected as an MP for the Liberal Party in 2015 in Ottawa Centre, Catherine McKenna involved her children in her campaign. Rather than trying to manage her family and career separately, she set about creating ways to blend them.

I just brought my kids everywhere. I built my campaign around the fact that I had kids. They're very outgoing, Madeline and Isabelle, so they came to everything. When I was canvassing, they would come with me. They loved the action. They would knock on doors then say, "Hi. We're Madeline and Isabelle, and our mom is here too. What are your issues?"

As minister, it's a much busier schedule, and I am sad my kids cannot do much of the travelling with me. In the campaign, kids in the community became involved in great ways. Parents seemed pleased to have a woman role model, and the kids pushed an innovative approach to the campaign. At one door, I ran into the former ballet teacher of one of my kids. She said how awesome it was that I was running and asked how she could help. This all led to a big flash mob dance choreographed by her with all the kids and parents out in front of my campaign headquarters the weekend before the election. The media loved it. The kids were energized, and the moms got involved in helping me win. The involvement of kids led to me thinking totally differently about what a campaign could look like.

" *I built my campaign around the fact I had kids.*

CHERI DINOVO

First elected to the Ontario Legislature as an MPP for Parkdale-High Park for the NDP in a by-election in 2006, Cheri DiNovo was re-elected in 2007, 2011, and 2014. Before DiNovo won the election, she was overwhelmed with the time and energy it took to win the nomination.

I grew up in a social justice household to characterize it. My father was a founding member of the NDP and was constantly volunteering for the party in downtown Toronto. So, I grew up essentially tagging along in one campaign after another. It was never his campaign, but my father was always working on another person's campaign. It was in the blood in that sense, going to demonstrations. It was just a part of my childhood.

Conversation around the dinner table was very political. Half my family on my mother's side were very staunch Conservatives. My father's side was NDP. There were always vibrant debates. The one thing they could agree on was that they didn't like Liberals. If anything, quite frankly, it probably didn't inspire me to get into politics as a teenager. But I came full circle some years later. Growing up in a family filled with political debate set a course for me.

You need to go into politics with a heads-up on the time it takes and the impact that it will have on your family. Running for nomination, I took a three-month leave from the church. I was stuffing envelopes at the kitchen table and making calls from my home. I kept being assured that things would get easier once I became the party candidate. They were right in some ways. The entire party machinery comes in behind you. But the all-consuming pace continued 12 hours a day. First, I was selling myself to the party; then, I was selling the party to the voters. It was like telemarketing constantly. The skill set is the same, but the circles keep widening, and the time dedicated to politics keeps filling every space.

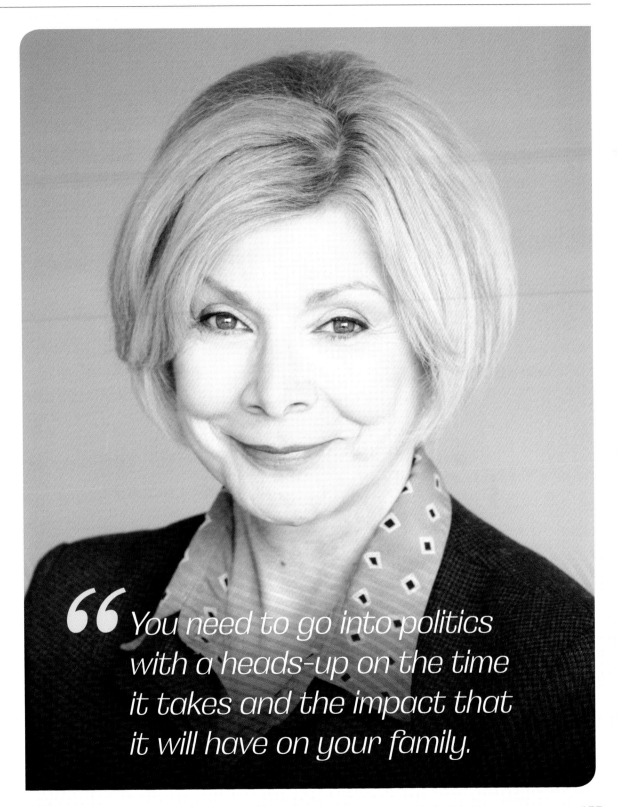

> *You need to go into politics with a heads-up on the time it takes and the impact that it will have on your family.*

CAROL HUGHES

Carol Hughes, elected as an MP for the NDP in 2008, had to think through her personal priorities before running for office. Hughes was re-elected as the MP for Algoma-Manitoulin-Kapuskasing in the following two federal elections.

Although I didn't win my first two elections in 2004 and 2006, I ran and got elected in 2008, 2011, and 2015. During my first two campaigns, we saw the votes increased for the NDP, and although I had done well in those campaigns, I wasn't planning to run a third time due to personal circumstances. My sister was diagnosed with Alzheimer's at just 50 years old, and so I had to rethink my priorities. We wanted to try and keep her in her own home for as long as possible, and so the decision was made for me to take a job transfer to Sudbury. There was a period of time that I was travelling between Sudbury and my home in Elliot Lake on the weekends with my sister. I had also applied for a job with the Canadian Labour Congress and was hired as their northern representative. At one point, my sister's children moved her into a long-term care home because of the progression of the disease.

At the start of my entry into politics, I had received several calls from the party to encourage me to run, including from Libby Davies. When I was asked to be the candidate again for the 2008 election, I was quite hesitant and received several more calls from the party, including from Jack Layton and Michael Lewis, who played important roles throughout my campaigns. On the day I was to give the answer, I got up that morning and said to my husband, "I'm going to say no to them." And he said, "Why?" And I said, "Chances are I'm going to get elected this time, and I'm not going to be home much." He said, "With your career with the Canadian Labour Congress, you're not home many hours anyway."

Although I still had a lot of family responsibilities, with the support of my husband, I decided: "Okay. I'll give it one more shot" — and in 2008 I was elected.

PHYLLIS WILLIAMS

Phyllis Williams, Chief of Curve Lake First Nation, acknowledges that her partner's role in their family has helped facilitate her work, not only in council but also throughout her career.

There are always personal sacrifices when you commit yourself to politics. I am so very blessed to have a partner who is my support when I can't be there for my family. He has always encouraged the work I do, wherever and whatever that might be.

This is how it has been my whole career life. He has supported me in every way you can imagine. He would ensure the children got to school in times of my absence. Our youngest daughter used to have the most unbalanced pigtails, but she would never complain. Together, we made it work and made possible my life in council and as Chief.

I am so very blessed to have a partner who is my support when I can't be there for my family.

New Directions

Over a thousand people were in the hall when the preferential balloting was taking place. Supporters of all three contestants were packed tightly in the arena chanting slogans while I shook hands with hundreds of strangers. I was first to fall off the ballot. I left right away to make it to my son's National Collegiate Athletic Association (NCAA) hockey play-offs. He was on the ice in the last period of the game. The puck bounced off the post, and he flicked it in. I caught him just as the team was loading onto the bus and told him news of the nomination loss: "Mom, some of my best goals have come from rebounds. I believe in you." In turning the page in politics, nothing has stayed with me quite so indelibly as those words.

The journey into and out of politics rarely follows a prescribed script. For some, victory leads to great heights, while others disappear at the nomination stage. The women featured in this book have run for a number of things — nomination, a seat, party leadership, and re-election among them; some have retired from politics at various points throughout the political process. While running for or while in office, personal priorities, health, or family matters can overtake the importance of work. A life in politics inevitably ends, but the skills acquired from time spent in the political arena will be invaluable in the move in a new direction.

JENNIFER HOLLETT

Jennifer Hollett, the federal NDP candidate for University-Rosedale in 2015, ran for Toronto city council in 2018 — the year that the premier, Doug Ford, cut city council from 47 ward councillors to 25 when the election campaign was underway.

In 2018, I declared I would be running for Toronto city council in a new ward that had been created after five years of consultation with citizens, given the growth of Toronto's population.

I had done my analysis prior to giving up my job at Twitter. There was a path to victory. Entering any election race takes serious consideration, weighing the pros and cons, the opportunities and risks. It was an exciting time in the city. There was a diverse cohort of progressive candidates running. There was a new ward. There was no incumbent. I decided to go. I let Twitter know, then entered the race full force, filed my papers, and paid the registration fee.

We had already begun fundraising and securing endorsements. We were building a strong team of volunteers. About two weeks into the race, we had great momentum and media attention. We hosted a kick-off party. It was in full swing when suddenly people began locking eyes and glancing at their text messages. My campaign manager pulled me aside to tell me the rumours. The premier of Ontario was about to introduce a bill (Bill 5) that would reduce the number of wards in Toronto city council — no other municipality in the province, just Toronto — almost halfway through the municipal race from 47 to 25 wards. Some candidates had dipped into savings, some had moved wards.

I ... announced I was not going to run.

A group of concerned citizens got together, and we sued the government of Ontario. The court case was moving very fast. Meanwhile, my campaign manager and I were trying to keep the campaign team on course, moving forward, all the while not knowing if the court case would be won. When we won the court case, that sent a huge wave of relief through us all. The citizens had been heard. Then — the case was stayed. The premier had his way. The wards would be reduced to 25.

We had to dig deep. We did not want this to turn into the "Hunger Games," where candidates of shared values were running against each other. There were countless huddles among candidates, texts, emails. I could run in a "new ward," but there were two incumbents, and that would put me up against a city councillor I respected and admired, and the only woman of colour and openly gay person on council. I went on CBC's Metro Morning and announced I was not going to run. I had made the decision to support Kristyn Wong-Tam.

> **My life remained political, just not in politics.**

LIBBY DAVIES

An activist for more than 40 years, Libby Davies has fought for social change from outside and inside the political system as a city councillor from 1982 to 1993 and an NDP parliamentarian from 1997 to 2015. In her memoir, *Outside In*, Davies took the opportunity, moving forward from politics, to analyze how change happens.

To be honest, it was an enormous relief. I had been in politics for five terms municipally and six terms federally. It felt like a very big chunk of my life. I timed my exit; it was my own decision.

I was so tired when it was all over. I had no idea how draining flying back and forth from Ottawa to BC was for 18 years — spending the weekends in the constituency attending events and meeting with people. It was gruelling. I had no idea the toll it had taken on me over time.

The first thing I did was sleep. A lot. I just slept. Then, like everyone else who "retires," I became busier than ever. I set my goal to write a political memoir. The phone started ringing, and people were asking if I might run for Vancouver mayor. I didn't, but I endorsed a candidate and got involved. I am a human rights and social justice activist. I always will be.

It never stops. I have stayed engaged in issues that I have always cared deeply about. My life remained political, just not in politics. It's a different role, and that suits me just fine.

ELENI BAKOPANOS

Eleni Bakopanos was first elected as an MP for Saint-Denis for the Liberal Party in 1993 and then, when the riding was merged with another, served as the MP for Ahuntsic from 1997 to 2006. She is the first Greek-born woman to be elected to Parliament.

The biggest and most unforeseen detour occurred in 1996 when I discovered that Saint-Denis had been merged with the riding of Papineau and no longer existed on the electoral map. After having worked so hard to be the candidate and win a huge majority, I questioned whether I would be a one-term MP. No one in the party had mentioned to me that Saint-Denis had been erased by the Electoral Boundaries Commission years earlier. I was heading into an election year in 1997 without a riding.

The riding on the north side of Saint-Denis, Ahuntsic, where I have lived since 1970, had been lost by the Liberals in 1993 and was held by the Bloc Québécois. Ahuntsic had a tradition of electing women; Jeanne Sauvé, the first woman to be Speaker of the House of Commons and Governor General of Canada, had held the riding for years and following her, another female Liberal MP had been elected. I knew the party wanted a "star candidate" (a term I dislike) to run in Ahuntsic. I said to them, "I can be that star. Watch me win back the riding!" In fact, many of the francophone voters knew my father, Johnny, from his delicious pizza, and when I knocked on their doors, I said I was Johnny's daughter. I believe it was one of the reasons I won a majority.

I questioned whether I would be a one-term MP.

I had always told my kids that achieving anything in life was all about grit.

TINA BEAUDRY-MELLOR

Tina Beaudry-Mellor lost the race to become a councillor on Regina City Council in 2012, but in 2016, she was elected as the MLA for the riding of Regina University as a member of the Saskatchewan Party.

My first defeat was a tough lesson. I had always told my kids that achieving anything in life was all about grit. It was an important mantra in my family. Anything you want you can get. You just need to "grit it out." When the kids saw how hard I worked to win my first election, and then they saw me get defeated, they wanted to know why. I really didn't have a good explanation.

On top of that, a defeat in politics is very public. Many other setbacks are more private. But election defeats are very public. There's no way around it. Your ego takes a hit.

With time, I came to appreciate the broader context. In most elections, people vote governments out. They want change. No matter how hard you work, this reality, combined with people's party loyalty, the performance of the leader, and the platform, determines the outcome in your riding.

It's a complicated explanation. But kids who play sports know that winning is often out of your hands. Politics is like that. It's a team sport.

Sometimes the things you think are the worst in life turn out to be the best.

ANITA VANDENBELD

After her initial bid for Parliament and loss in the 2011 federal election, Anita Vandenbeld changed direction and accepted two different positions overseas. In 2015, Vandenbeld was elected as an MP for the Liberal Party for Ottawa West-Nepean.

I lost the 2011 election. The day after the election, I lost status and standing [in the party], as other candidates lose standing. You disappear. One minute you have the entire party apparatus behind you, and the next you are alone.

I closed the campaign, wrote the thank-you notes, and then went away for six months to the Democratic Republic of the Congo to a fantastic job as a resident director with the National Democratic Institute (NDI). I then took a two-year assignment with UNDP in Bangladesh. I realized that this decision would bring me back only one year before the next federal election [in 2015]. But I just could not financially put my life on hold.

Six months into my position in Bangladesh, I became very ill. I had to be evacuated back to Canada. By that time, the party was into the leadership cycle, and things were very energetic. That's when I decided, "Yes, I am going to run again." I also met the man who is now my husband. The fact is, had I not gotten so sick, I likely would have been discouraged enough by the politics and not run a second time. My detour overseas came to a halt. I ran for nomination, then Parliament. And I won. Sometimes the things you think are the worst in life turn out to be the best.

ANNE MCLELLAN

Anne McLellan entered federal politics in 1993 and held a series of cabinet positions for the Liberal Party throughout her time as an MP. McLellan won four consecutive terms by thin margins for Edmonton Northwest, West, and Centre.

You need to think of politics as public service. ... Anyone who thinks politics is a career is making a mistake in my view.

Y ou need to think of politics as public service. Running for office, being a member of Parliament, and if you are very lucky, serving in cabinet is not a career. It is taking time out from your career — law in my case — to do public service. Anyone who thinks politics is a career is making a mistake in my view.

There certainly are things you can accomplish from the platform of politics. But politics is time-dated. In my case, it was 12 years of service. It was time out from my academic career to represent my riding and achieve some goals. I won my first election by 11 votes. Several cycles and successes later, it was over. My teams at the minister's office, the Hill, and the constituency office dispersed quickly. This was their livelihood. They moved on quickly. But a small core of us met monthly over dinner with lots of wine to wistfully look back and remember the terrific times we shared while it lasted. It took at least six months of "dinner therapy" to help us all move on.

Another type of defeat, although I was lucky enough never to experience it, was to be removed from cabinet. You lose a lot of profile and support. In those moments, it is important to remember, you are in Parliament to represent your riding. You are their voice. That's at the root of your service. Your constituency gave you the chance to serve.

I knew the end would come at some point. If you don't, you shouldn't go into politics.

MARY CLANCY

After serving as an MP for the Liberal Party in Halifax from 1988 to 1997, Mary Clancy was defeated in the 1997 federal election by NDP leader Alexa McDonough. The National Film Board's *Why Women Run* documents this race and describes it as one of the most contested races in the country that election.

I knew the end would come at some point. If you don't, you shouldn't go into politics. You can be so involved, then bang. It's all over. It was an extraordinary nine years. No other life experience could have equalled it. Picking up the pieces, I spent some days with my Halifax and Ottawa staff, cleaned out my desks, then stepped out of elected politics.

I was sorry I lost the election. I would miss Parliament and the cut and thrust of politics, yes, of course, but I am, thank God, not subject to depression, even during life events much more crushing than losing an election. I was delighted with the prime minister's trust in me and looking forward to a new challenge. Plus, I was immediately swamped with preparation for the briefings that would commence August, including an intensive tour of the Maritimes, Ontario, and Quebec. There was no time for any regrets.

I was with a colleague at the swearing-in of cabinet that fall. Several colleagues asked me, "What's next?" There was a job relating to the Status of Women that several members of the public service asked me to apply for. I was reasonably sure that something was coming when I was told by one cabinet minister, "Mary, you are not aiming high enough."

I was extremely fortunate when I got a phone call from the prime minister right after the first cabinet meeting after the swearing-in offering me the post in New England as Consul General of Canada. It served as a bridge to life post-politics. I was one of the lucky ones. Back in Halifax later, after a successful term in Boston, I re-engaged in community causes, and I always keep the phone on the hook for mentoring women entering politics.

MARY SMITH

Mary Smith was elected to Lakefield council in Ontario as deputy reeve in 1998; she went on to serve on city council and as deputy reeve for Smith-Ennismore-Lakefield. Smith then served as Selwyn mayor from 2010 to 2018 and Peterborough County Deputy Warden from 2016 to 2018 before retiring.

You need to know when it's time to close a door.

When I was moderating a panel on women in politics, I advised women to run to win. Don't run to get your message out. Run a technical, strategic campaign, and run to win. And get in shape. Politics is very physically demanding. Especially in rural areas, you cover a lot of distance. Be smart, work with a driver, and wear practical footwear. When I had a stress fracture in my leg when I was running for the mayor position in 2010, I had 40 volunteers doing phone canvassing so that the campaign was able to keep going.

When you run municipally, you control your own policy and develop your own brand. It's exciting and demanding. You need to get attuned to your electorate. It's not intuitive. It takes practice and constant two-way communication to be a candidate, elected official, community leader, and change-maker.

When I was deciding whether to run for a ward seat or across the whole municipality at large, I spoke with my father, who had 40 years of experience as a member of municipal council. He was a man of few words. He said, "Well, it's always nicer to win." It was his way of saying that I should run where I was more likely to win. It helped me decide where and when to run. It was sage advice. And, over a fulfilling number of elected terms, I must admit, it's been pleasant to win. But we all have our best-before date. I always say that there are four ways to leave politics: you can retire, you can run and lose, you might die in office, and there are those who get jailed for an offence. I prefer the first option. I think you need to know when it's time to close a door, and I believe another door always opens.

You can't live life in the rear-view mirror.

DEB GREY

Deb Grey became the first Reform Party MP in 1989 and became deputy leader in 1993. The Reform Party became the Canadian Alliance Party in 2000. Grey was later named Leader of the Official Opposition, the first woman in Canadian history to have this position.

You go to Ottawa, and you think you are famous. I drove my motorcycle to the Hill. They coined me "Gladiator Grey." I was the only one of our party sitting in the House of Commons. I became a household name across the country. But I always made a point of phoning back home frequently to keep my primary relationships alive. Life in politics ends. You don't want to go home and say to your friends, "Hey, remember me?" And have them reply, "No. I don't, really."

When politics ended, my salary went to zero overnight. Staff disappeared practically the next day. All of a sudden, you're writing your own letters, sorting your own files, paying your own bills. Your official cellphone is cancelled. You book and buy your own plane tickets. Remember how long that took? Welcome back to reality. You buy your own stamps. Repair your own computer. All those things that underpinned your efficiency disappear overnight.

You disappear pretty quickly. I left in June 2004. The next Christmas, not six months later, a former staffer phoned me: "Deb, we're in the Hall of Honour at the Conservative Christmas Party. Where are you?" I had to say I didn't get the invitation. Life on the Hill is busy. It moves on rapidly without you. You can't live life in the rear-view mirror. You can waste a lot of energy looking backwards.

Leaving politics was not a surprise for me. I had planned it. I announced it one year ahead. Even then, the shock set in. I was 52. Everyone had been saying I was so famous that my phone would ring off the hook with offers to use my talent. It didn't. So, I sat down, wrote a book, *Never Retreat, Never Explain, Never Apologize: My Life in Politics*, then turned the corner.

It's important to remember the things that keep you grounded and going forward. For me, that's family, friends, my church, and my motorcycle!

CAMMIE JAQUAYS

After attending the 2014 Liberal Biennial Convention in Montreal, Cammie Jaquays, a professor, decided to launch her nomination bid for MP. After ten months, she made the difficult decision to withdraw and place her support behind another candidate.

Many talented and committed individuals get lost in the dynamics of "party win" politics. I was among them.

Nominations are all about the win. People enter politics with the idea that they can make a difference, change the world, and make the country a better place. While this is true, the goal of a nomination for the party is to secure that person who will win the riding in the next election.

We're a timed society. When teaching, there is a well-defined timeline for students and instructors. You know when a course is over. You mark exams, and that's it. This is not the case in a nomination. Those of us with families and a career face terrific challenges mounting and sustaining campaigns and caring for a family when the finish line is unannounced, and the goalpost keeps changing. The nomination date is set by the party (seemingly randomly but surely strategically), and you never know when the nomination will be called.

I first entered the federal race to bring a strong voice to local politics. For 10 months, I put enormous effort into my campaign with a great team, working daily to reach more and more people, selling more than 500 memberships, which would have garnered a win in many ridings across Canada. I was in the lead, but the timing of the nomination kept being delayed, and my competitor, a popular high school teacher, took the lead, and I slid into second place. When I realized I did not have enough new members signed up to guarantee the nomination personally, it was time for a strategic move.

The Liberals were third in the polls nationally at the time, months out from the federal election. A local woman, Maryam Monsef, had just run for mayor, having built significant local momentum with her signs and debates, despite her loss. I have long been a proponent of women in politics, and I felt her chances to take the nomination and carry the riding were good. So, I made a decision to give the party a better chance in the local riding. I stepped aside and invited Maryam to enter the race. For the party, it was all about the "win." Many talented and committed individuals get lost in the dynamics of party "win" politics. I was among them.

JEANNETTE MONTUFAR

Before running for office, Jeannette Montufar was a professor in the Faculty of Engineering – Civil Engineering at the University of Manitoba. When Montufar, a PC candidate, was defeated in the 2016 provincial election in Manitoba, her career took a very different turn.

After being defeated, I needed space.

We were not considered a target riding — meaning one likely to win. We were unofficially referred to as an orphan riding. It was basically just the six of us doing all the door knocking. There were two others, an official agent and an engineer. All of us had full-time jobs. We had to optimize our time.

We didn't have extensive networks or an MLA going door to door with us. So, we set about designing our own system. I'm very proud of it. We managed to knock on every door six times. My campaign manager was the engineer doing all the computer-driven organization and lists. He designed a canvassing system to use every ounce of our energy and time to best advantage. Nothing is more basic to democracy than politics on the doorstep. His system put our campaign on almost every doorstep in a fast-paced, high-energy campaign.

After being defeated, I needed space. I had to put distance between myself and the intense experience of politics. The campaign with its challenges and the ups and downs left me feeling I needed a different path. I got very involved in cycling. I used to cycle quite a bit.

I left the university six months after the election. I was a tenured, full professor. It came as a shock to everyone. Why would somebody in their right mind quit their ideal job? I thought a lot about it, and I realized that I was not happy there because the job simply became too easy. I could not imagine spending the rest of my career as a professor.

So here I am, a businesswoman. There was some issue that I had been very partisan and political. That brought some negative consequences. They eventually ironed out.

The Minister of Status of Women appointed me chair of a Women's Advisory Council to ensure gender equality in Manitoba and to provide advice on social, health, political, and economic issues for women in the province. That completely motivated me. That injected life into me, to be at the table, because I thought I could make a difference.

DEB SCHULTE

Deb Schulte served as a regional councillor for the City of Vaughan from 2010 to 2014; in 2015, she was elected as the MP for the Liberal Party in King-Vaughan, Ontario.

Enter politics with an open mind for its challenges and difficulties, and appreciate the temporal position of privilege you occupy.

Politics is not a career. Expect it to end. Give it your all, knowing that you've got influence for a limited time. Never forget the people who worked to get you there. Understand just how lucky you are to have the privilege of a position of influence.

Many people fought and worked hard to get elected. Timing and the election cycle did not favour them. Others won one election, then lost the next. Be careful not to let your ego get the best of you or to pin all your life on politics. When you're out, you're out. It all ends swiftly. I have been there.

When you win, know you are a part of a much larger team. There's a whole lot of members grinding away on committees. Only a tiny fraction of the people elected are in cabinet. All of us are a cog in the large wheel of the parliamentary process. At the centre of our MP life is our home constituency. You need to keep your focus constantly on the people who placed their trust in you. Enter politics with an open mind for its challenges and difficulties, and appreciate the temporal position of privilege you occupy. Politics is service.

CELINA CAESAR-CHAVANNES

Celina Caesar-Chavannes became an MP for the Liberal Party in Whitby, Ontario, in 2015, and left the Liberal caucus March 2019 to sit as an Independent.

I tell my kids all the time to know who they are and to trust their personal worth. "Make mistakes, go ahead, please. That is what they are designed for. But then, you have to learn from those mistakes."

When you trip and fall flat on your face, you may feel like you can't get up. Sometimes you just have to lie there. At the very least, just turn over. Just roll over, and look up at the sky. Stay as long as you want, but just turn over, and start looking up. And then, when you are ready — which the stories in this book will help you do — get the courage to get back up and stand up straight.

Some people say, "Pick yourself up, dust yourself off, and start all over again." That's not usually how it works. Sometimes you have to just lie there. Then, if you can, roll over, and pick yourself up.

Success means different things to different people. The most successful thing you can do for yourself is to be authentically you. Bending too far, you can break. When people criticize aspects of me and if I bend to change who I am, it never lasts long. Be authentically you, and the world will begin to see that authenticity. Don't try to adapt yourself to fit the world. Let the world around you fit you in your authentic, breathable self. Secrets are so difficult to keep, lies are impossible. Trust your own worth.

> *Let the world around you fit you in your authentic, breathable self. ... Trust your own worth.*

Part 4

A WORLD MADE
ANEW

*C*anadian women in politics, including the many trailblazers in *Women on the Ballot*, have been important change-makers, as their stories illustrate. As I reflect on the women's stories, however, it's clear that achieving equality isn't just about representation — it's about creating meaningful change. While reaching gender parity in politics is important, even more important is the difference women bring to government — in outlook and in action. Women's voices and experiences change the political culture; diversity in politics changes the conversation and shifts priorities.

In 1975, Marilyn Waring was elected as an MP for the National Party in New Zealand at age 23. In 1984, she supported the Opposition's anti-nuclear bill — the prime minister, leader of the National Party, called an election in response, and lost. New Zealand became a "nuclear-free zone." In March 2019, 35 years later, after a mass shooting at two mosques in New Zealand that claimed 50 lives, Prime Minister Jacinda Ardern changed the country's gun laws within six days. The UN has stated the following: "The evidence is clear: wherever women take part in a peace process, peace lasts longer … a peace agreement, which includes women, is 35 percent more likely to last at least 15 years."

In Canada, many women in politics are bringing about change. Elizabeth May is recognized around the world for her leadership on the environment, Chrystia Freeland's work on feminist foreign policy sets a new standard, and RoseAnne Archibald's work with the Assembly of First Nations in support of women are all testament to the difference that women can make.

Throughout the interviews, four major themes surfaced when discussing the difference between parity and equality: the importance of making women's history visible; feminism and politics; creating enduring change; and the fact that representation is more than just numbers. The first theme focuses on the "missing figures" in the narrative of Canada's history and democracy, and speaks to the importance of building civic literacy in schools. The second theme highlights the women's experiences with feminism and politics while "creating enduring change" discusses systemic discrimination and introduces the analytical tools and democratic reforms that can help tackle it beyond the whims of electoral cycles — including gender-based analysis plus (GBA +), gender-responsive budgeting (GRB), and electoral reform. Finally, in a call for women to put their names on the ballot, the women interviewed for this book spoke about the many ways domestically and internationally that parity in politics was much more than just numbers — women's presence in politics was building a new world.

Daughters of the Vote delegates, part of International Women's Day, in the House of Commons on Parliament Hill in Ottawa on 8 March 2017

Making Herstory Visible

Democracy is a system that relies on respect for the law, freedom of political expression, and civic participation. People around the world have fought for, defended, and died for the freedom to be governed by democratic principles: rule by the people through fair and free elections. Teaching democracy is a cornerstone to keeping it. However, recorded history often overlooks women's contributions ("herstory").

In Canada, women's history begins with Indigenous women. Accounts of Canadian history must accurately reflect the history of First Nations and the nature of Confederation, including the Indian Residential Schools Settlement Agreement and the Truth and Reconciliation Commission (TRC). Programs such as "Dancing Backwards" and "Facing History and Ourselves" provide Canadian classrooms with templates for exploring female role models in the political life of Canada and for teaching Canadian history in an exciting, engaging manner. These programs help to instill in young people an appreciation of the role of women in keeping democracy in Canada strong.

RUTH ELLEN BROSSEAU

Ruth Ellen Brosseau, MP for Berthier-Maskinongé in Quebec for the NDP, became Whip of the NDP in 2019.

I was thrilled to be in schools making visible the role of women in politics to young students. While it's usually the teacher that prepares the students, sometimes I see that the Grade 6 and Grade 7 students have the best questions. I remember being stumped a few times by them.

The teacher delivers a part of the curriculum where students talk about provincial and federal politics. Then, I talk to them about my personal experience. It's a part of making women visible and politics personal.

My staff also instigated a McGill shadow day ["Women in the House"]. Every year, McGill has women come to Parliament and shadow female MPs. It's amazing to get to spend the day with a young student. She sees a day in the life of an MP. It gives her a good insight of what it's like. Equal Voice did this on a national scale with Daughters of the Vote. It was such a touching moment to be up in the gallery and just see the House full of young women and listening to their statements. I had goosebumps.

> *I was thrilled to be in schools making visible the role of women in politics to young students.*

ALEXA MCDONOUGH

Alexa McDonough has served as the leader of Nova Scotia's provincial NDP, as MLA, as leader of the federal NDP, and as an MP. In 2009, after leaving politics, McDonough was appointed the interim president of Mount Saint Vincent University in Halifax.

A question that concerns me deeply is this: "Why do we do so little about political literacy in our school systems?" It is pathetic how little we Canadians do in our school system to learn about democracy. Political literacy is foundational in countries aspiring to be democratic. It is the exception to be in a school that teaches courses in civics and politics across all grades and to all students. It is neither systematic nor required. How alarming is that?

I worked with the organization of former parliamentarians for quite a while. I was always pushing for the need to do more about political literacy in Canada. I think we should start this as soon as students enter school and keep building it through the curriculum across all grades. In addition to teaching political literacy, it is important to have model parliaments and actively engage students in the democratic process. Many who have gone on to run politically in Canada first experienced a model UN or model parliaments during their high school years. Unfortunately, these experiences are anecdotal; they depend on individual teachers having the commitment to organize these events on top of their teaching loads. It is seriously alarming that this is left to chance. Democracy should not be an extracurricular activity.

Why do we do so little about political literacy in our school systems?

> **Most Canadians don't know our history and don't know how strong and powerful Indigenous women are.**

AMANDA LATHLIN

Amanda Lathlin became the first First Nations woman to be elected to the Manitoba Legislative Assembly in 2015 as an MLA for The Pas for the NDP.

Indigenous culture respects and honours its Elders. Their knowledge and wisdom guide us. I've spoken often about those who came before me — my great-grandmother, my grandmother, and mother. Most Canadians may not know just how resilient and strong Indigenous women are. We draw upon our ancestry. They are woven into the fabric of our community and decision-making. In turbulent moments, I spiritually call upon that ancestry. I always teach Indigenous women, especially girls, about coming from that strength. I do believe it is a key component of understanding your own self-worth. We do not pass over older members of our community. We draw upon their strength and our lineage. Spending just a few hours with Elders and women who have gone before me rejuvenates me.

By 2017, we had four Indigenous women in the Manitoba Legislature. We all have similar stories. In fact, we have sat in committee crying, listening, and sharing very similar stories.

The fastest-growing segment of the Canadian population is the Indigenous population. At a time in our history when there are so many university graduates, a large number of them are Indigenous women with children. It is important to bring Aboriginal women's culture and perspective into education.

Most Canadians don't know our history and don't know how strong and powerful Indigenous women are. It is important our school systems integrate this Indigenous perspective in telling our history. This is an important step towards reconciliation in Canada. We are in an era of reconciliation. The Truth and Reconciliation report has 94 calls to action. I carry that *Call to Action* booklet in my pocket. It is the size of my hand. It is a daily reference. I have it every time I am on the floor of the legislature to relate government policy to actions towards reconciliation.

I always teach Indigenous women, especially girls, about our heritage and that strength and being able to draw upon that strength and that lineage and ancestry. A part of this process of educating and informing ourselves is weaving our stories into politics. For example, when Melanie Mark was elected as the first Indigenous woman MLA in British Columbia, she was drummed into the legislature with Elders — something I wish I had done. I shared her pride. I cried watching her dance to the drums. She was the first Indigenous woman MLA in BC as I was the first Indigenous woman MLA in Manitoba in 2015. It took us 99 years.

I was a little girl when I watched my father, Oscar Lathlin, Chief of the Opaskwayak Cree Nation, during his role with the inquiry into the murder of Helen Betty Osborne in the 1980s. My father went on to become MLA when I was 15 years old. He was MLA for 18 years representing The Pas. He was my biggest role model. He had a profound influence. He is why I am here today as an MLA. It is an honour to follow in his footsteps.

ELIZABETH MAY

An environmentalist, writer, activist, and lawyer, Elizabeth May has been active in the environmental movement since the 1970s. The leader of the Green Party and MP for the Vancouver Island riding of Saanich-Gulf Islands, May believes that schools should be teaching the history of women in Canada.

Schools should be teaching herstory.

We really need to have girls in school know more about our history, when women won the vote, and women's emerging role in politics today. Schools should be teaching herstory. Our young people need to learn how much effort it took for women to be recognized.

I think we have forgotten the historical importance of the Persons Case. We forget how hard it was for women to get the vote. Agnes Macphail was the first woman to be an MP. We tend to forget, or never learn, about the trailblazers. It is living but lost history. Schools should teach the battles fought just to be recognized as persons, to be able to vote in elections, and to be seen as serious players. It puts things into a fresh perspective.

I think that we need to start educating people to look at everything through a woman's lens as well as a lens of diversity and First Nations.

LENORE ZANN

Lenore Zann was first elected to the Nova Scotia Legislature as an MLA for Truro-Bible Hill in 2009 and re-elected in 2013 and 2017 as MLA for the renamed Truro-Bible Hill-Millbrook-Salmon River for the NDP.

I think that we need to start educating people to look at everything through a woman's lens as well as a lens of diversity and First Nations. Consider Canada's Mi'kmaq communities in Nova Scotia. I admire friends like Cheryl Maloney, law graduate, hockey mom, former band councillor, and president of the Native Women's Association. Cheryl has spent a lot of time trying to educate non-Native people about the treaties that were signed between colonists and the Mi'kmaq — especially since they never sold or leased their lands to the newcomers. Instead they signed "Peace and Friendship Treaties" allowing the newcomers to share their lands in peace and friendship — but they still owned the land. This is why many Nova Scotians now acknowledge we are on the "unceded" Mi'kmaq territory. Cheryl and others have also been instrumental in protecting her community from plans by the Calgary-based AltaGas company to pour hundreds of millions of litres of salt brine daily into the Shubenacadie River near Stewiacke, Nova Scotia, in order to carve out salt caverns to store natural gas. Yet the river is the last remaining spawning ground for the endangered striped sea bass that the Mi'kmaq have fished for thousands of years.

Other proud Mi'kmaq women have also been fighting for Mother Earth in Nova Scotia, and I'm proud to stand with them shoulder to shoulder and hand in hand as a woman and as NDP Spokesperson for the Environment, Status of Women, and Aboriginal Affairs.

Women who are politicians can, and should, partner with Indigenous women and lift up their voices with their sisters to help them be heard. We need to educate ourselves and our children about First Nations environmental leadership, stewardship, rights, and treaties — but also to develop a simple appreciation and love for the land, air, water, wild creatures, and life itself. After all we are all one. That's why I and my Mi'kmaq friends say, "Wela'lin" (Thank you).

SHEILA COPPS

Sheila Copps served as MPP for Hamilton Centre from 1981 to 1984 for the Ontario Liberal Party and as an MP for Hamilton East from 1984 to 2004 for the federal Liberal Party. Copps was Deputy Prime Minister and Minister of Canadian Heritage from 1996 to 2003.

School curriculums are provincial jurisdictions. When I was Minister of Heritage, we created a Council of Ministers and promoted a clearing house of history to promote a national common identity and a common understanding of history. We started creating pedagogical kits, including kits that included stories about Parliament and the Canadian flag. It was available to download from the Internet for teachers. It was not gender-specific then. It should be now.

Politics is part of civic engagement.

Youth get most of their information from the Internet, and cyberspaces are a lot more open. Youth should have the vote at 16, and we should allow political clubs in high schools. We have all kinds of other clubs, but not for civics and democracy. Politics is part of civic engagement. School books and materials should have stories on women in politics. Lowering the voting age, introducing material on women in politics into the curriculum, and going to Internet voting would all enhance youth engagement in democracy.

ISABEL METCALFE

Isabel Metcalfe was the Liberal candidate for Carleton-Mississippi Mills in Ontario in the 2006 federal election and ran for councillor of Ward 17 in the 2010 Ottawa municipal election. In 2018, Metcalfe was celebrated for her contribution to the Ottawa chapter of the Famous Five.

I have been deeply involved in the Famous Five initiative in Canada. Placing statues in public places is important to remind our country of the watershed moments when women worked to be recognized as persons.

If you measure the number of portraits and statues in public places conveying images of the change-makers to children, it becomes quickly apparent that images of women are largely missing. It is a form of public education, and I committed myself to helping make the Famous Five a part of our public spaces. It is equally important to keep this history present in schoolbooks and an important part of our political literacy. I remember Sheila Copps pushing the Famous Five Foundation to invest in schools. Young girls and boys need to see the complete picture.

Placing statues in public places is important to remind our country of the watershed moments when women worked to be recognized as persons.

PAT CARNEY

In 1980, Pat Carney became the first woman elected MP for Vancouver Centre and the first woman PC MP ever elected in BC. Carney served as an MP from 1980 to 1988 and was appointed to the Senate in 1990, retiring in 2008. Carney was the first PC senator from British Columbia since 1931.

Women's history and extraordinary contributions often get lost from history.

During my tenure as president of the Treasury Board, I initiated a Task Force on Barriers to Women in the Public Service, [whose report] *Beneath the Veneer* was a role model for other countries.

I personally interviewed Bertha Wilson, the first woman appointed to the Supreme Court of Canada. She told me how women have to prove themselves repeatedly while men bring their credentials with them.

An essential part of promoting and increasing women's leadership is ensuring they receive full credit for their hard work. It is often the case that women's achievements are attributed to others. Women's history and extraordinary contributions often get lost from history. We fail women when their hard work — getting "boney fingers" by knocking on the door and breaking down barriers — [is not recognized]. What is the point in getting boney fingers if it all falls out of sight and is not a permanent part of public record? Others often lay claim to the credit.

Making sure that women are planted firmly on the political landscape in leadership roles and ensuring their achievements are recorded accurately in the history books are an important part of keeping the record straight and successfully recruiting women into politics. Women deserve recognition of their achievements in political leadership in Canada.

Feminism and Politics

Women who lived through the 1960s and 1970s — Woodstock, the Vietnam War, the civil rights movement, and the women's liberation movement — may have a different view of feminism from that of third- or fourth-generation feminists. In 1975, the UN launched the first International Women's Day and declared the United Nations Decade for Women. Twenty years later, in 1995, tens of thousands of women from around the world converged in Beijing for the UN's Fourth World Conference on Women. It was electrifying. I was there. The Beijing Platform for Action was adopted by the delegations of all participating nations as a tool for transformative change. The platform became the cornerstone of a global agreement — entering the next millennium — on actions to achieve the equality and empowerment of women. As part of the ratification of the UN's Beijing Platform for Action, the government of Canada committed to using gender-based analysis plus (GBA+) to advance gender equality in Canada.

Feminism has continued to evolve over the decades since this conference in Beijing as these legal frameworks materialized. This evolution reflects the reality that gender intersects with many other identities, including race, sexual orientation, and faith. Today, gender equality is enshrined in the Charter of Rights and Freedoms in the Constitution of Canada. This means that people of all genders have the right to participate fully in all spheres of Canadian life and the right to an inclusive and democratic society. The women I interviewed for this book, whose entry into politics occurred over the last five decades (starting with Hazel McCallion, who was first elected in 1968), spoke of their experiences with feminism.

FARHEEN KHAN

Farheen Khan ran as the federal NDP candidate for Mississauga Centre in 2015. As the only hijab-wearing woman to run in the campaign, Khan details the connections between her faith and her feminism.

I am a feminist and a Muslim feminist. I do not believe that they are mutually exclusive.

I am a feminist and a Muslim feminist. I do not believe that they are mutually exclusive. Everyone has the right to self-determination, to their belief, and to wear what they choose. There is something to be said about standing for feminism. A woman should participate in all aspects of society and earn equivalent wages. As a Muslim, I take this one step further. As a woman of faith, I translate it to my religion. I ask how we can ensure organized religion is more gender-equitable. We are told gender equality is implicit in religion, but the practice of institutions may differ from that principle. So, I take my feminism and apply it to life, my time in politics, and to another level — my faith.

MICHELLE REMPEL

Michelle Rempel was elected as an MP in Calgary Centre-North in 2011 and Calgary Nose Hill in 2015, both for the Conservative Party. She has served as Minister of State (Western Economic Diversification) and as parliamentary secretary to the Minister of the Environment.

Feminism does not have a party affiliation.

Absolutely, 100% I am a feminist. That means to me integrating a gender perspective into all policy decision-making and removing gender barriers to the advancement of women in society. When I wrote a piece on sexism, people were shocked that a Conservative was a feminist. Feminism is often linked to left-leaning parties. For me, I look at policymaking through a feminist lens regardless of political ideology. Feminism does not have a party affiliation.

Each time I consider the advancement of women's rights, I ask myself what public policy would be effective. Is this a good use of taxpayer money? What are the options? It might be that government policy provides the best option to support parents through childcare facilities or a tax incentive. I also ask how policies could help men become fully involved in breaking stereotypes to support fathers staying home with newborn babies or income splitting. When I was attacked for not being a "real feminist," I felt like my legitimacy as a feminist was taken away because of my political affiliation. Feminism does not belong to any political party. We all share the vision.

CATHERINE FIFE

Catherine Fife was elected as the MPP for Waterloo for the NDP in 2012. Prior to her election, Fife served as trustee and chair of the Waterloo Region District School Board, vice president of the Canadian School Boards' Association, and president of the Ontario Public School Boards' Association.

Yes, I am a feminist. But I define this concept in terms of intersectionality. By this I mean that the fight for human rights and the protection of these rights under the Canadian Charter must be seen in broad terms. Gender equity is larger than gender parity. It is much more than just the numbers. The GBA+ tool enables politicians to see the impacts of their decisions on different groups of people. Equity applies to human rights for all, including gender, race, and ethnicity among the many identities people share.

> *Gender equity is larger than gender parity.*

MORGANE OGER

In 2016, Morgane Oger won the NDP nomination and ran in the 2017 BC provincial election. After her defeat, she assumed the role as chair of the Trans Alliance Society and was a member of the City of Vancouver's LGBTQ2+ Advisory Committee.

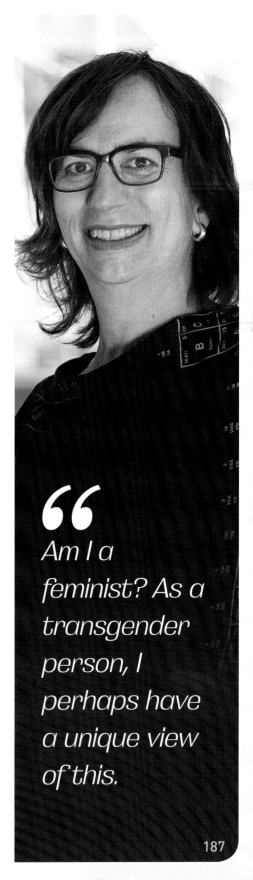

A m I a feminist? As a transgender person, I perhaps have a unique view of this. I very quickly noticed in politics that all of my fans were women at the nomination level. Women understand inequality far better than men. Men haven't experienced inequality to the same degree and don't as easily see and understand their advantage. Younger men understand better than older men who are entrenched in power structures. Men under 40 or so seem to have greater sympathy. For a long time, I presented as a man. I was socialized as a man. People perceived me as a man. So, to some degree, I had a type of window on how people behave differently towards men versus women. Did I feel that advantage as a man? That's complicated because did I ever feel like a man? There remain hurdles to open opportunities for all. All that said, of course I am a feminist.

> " *Am I a feminist? As a transgender person, I perhaps have a unique view of this.*

NIKI ASHTON

MP for Churchill-Keewatinook Aski, Manitoba, Niki Ashton was first elected in 2008. She ran for leadership of the NDP in 2012 at the age 29, the youngest on the list of contenders. Ashton was re-elected in 2015 and announced her second run for the NDP leadership in 2017.

Absolutely, I am a feminist — an intersectional feminist. For me there is no other way to be. From a young age, I knew how important feminist analysis and a feminist approach to living was. We believe in equality, justice for women, removing barriers of sexism, and confronting misogyny.

I've been finishing my PhD on millennial feminism, and I gained a lot of inspiration from younger feminists who are fighting for causes that are so critical — including sexual violence, environmental destruction, and the Black Lives Matter movement. Intersectional feminism is a tool for us all to move forward and to call out the systems that are holding us back.

For me, feminism is more than just increasing the numbers of women in elected office and leadership. Feminism means promoting a feminist agenda and inserting women's issues into the party platform. What's really necessary is not just identifying as a woman, but having a strong feminist agenda whose goal is to achieve equality and justice.

> *Feminism means promoting a feminist agenda and inserting women's issues into the party platform.*

> *For me, [feminism] means equal access, equal opportunity, and advocating for the dismantling of patriarchal structures in society.*

NICOLE SARAUER

In 2012, Nicole Sarauer was elected trustee for the Regina Catholic School Division. In 2016, she was elected to the Legislative Assembly of Saskatchewan for Regina Douglas Park and was interim leader of the Saskatchewan NDP from 2017 to 2018.

Definitely, I call myself a feminist. Feminism is not a word that I fear. I think anyone who believes that women are entitled to equality should also have no problem calling themselves feminists. For me, this means equal access, equal opportunity, and advocating for the dismantling of patriarchal structures in society. This includes also recognizing that faith institutions may not be fully reflective of this principle, but for me, that does not disqualify my faith. I can try to change the structures, but I do not mix the messenger with the message.

> *Absolutely, I consider myself a feminist. ... Just because you're a girl, you shouldn't be held back from doing anything.*

LISA RAITT

Lisa Raitt, three-time MP for the Conservative Party and Deputy Leader of the Official Opposition, believes in the power of education for girls' empowerment.

Absolutely, I consider myself a feminist. That is how I grew up. The Sisters of the Congregation of Notre Dame gave me my foundation. They taught me that you can do anything as long as you get an education. They were very big on educating girls. Once you got education, you could do anything. That was their message. So, that's the kind of feminist I am. Just because you're a girl, you shouldn't be held back from doing anything. With education, girls should not have to face barriers based on their gender. There shouldn't be any barriers for girls. Where there are, we should acknowledge the barriers and break them down.

LINDA DUNCAN

Linda Duncan is the only MP in Alberta representing the NDP. She was elected in 2008, 2011, and 2015 and announced that she will "pass the torch" in the next election.

I n earlier years, I worked on women's issues and helped form the National Action Committee on the Status of Women. I did all kinds of work with crisis centres in the early years of my career. Then I changed my primary focus to be on the environment. Of course, it doesn't matter what field you're in; there are gender implications and inequities. Overseas, the gender barriers to women are daunting. In our NDP caucus, we have a clear commitment to advance gender. We assign lead people to champion this portfolio, but gender is in all our respective files.

TINA BEAUDRY-MELLOR

Tina Beaudry-Mellor was elected as the MLA for Regina University in 2016 for the Saskatchewan Party. Prior to being elected, she served as the Saskatchewan chair of Equal Voice and was on the national board. To Beaudry-Mellor, feminism is about taking action.

I get asked all the time if I am a feminist. I have always struggled with the word because feminism means so many different things to different people. There's liberal feminism, social feminism, ecofeminism, radical feminism. For me, being a feminist is about action — it's about what you do. It's about dealing with the ways that patriarchy has oppressed not just women but also oppressed men into their very tight gendered jackets. These roles do not fit people's day-to-day lives today or their fluidity of character. If you've done the Bem Sex Role Inventory exercise, very few people end up on the full masculine or full feminine end of the spectrum. Sometimes I don't think feminism captures that aspect. I also think that some of the major policy discussions that we have as women in politics certainly circle around the issues of family and politics.

NAHANNI FONTAINE

Nahanni Fontaine is Ojibway from the Sagkeeng Anishinaabe First Nation. She was elected as the MLA for St. Johns in Manitoba for the NDP in 2016 and was named the House Leader of the Official Opposition in 2019.

In a First Nations context, you don't necessarily have discussions on feminism. We wear many different hats as women. I'm good to say I'm a feminist, but I rarely use that expression. In many respects, being an Indigenous woman or being an Indigenous person doesn't mesh with the term.

As a mother of two sons, I loathe the narrative of women versus men. When my son was born, my first thought was that he was a gift of the Creator. In the moment of birth, we are the closest to Creator we will ever be. The baby is a perfect and innocent creation. That is how everyone starts life. It was the most profound teaching of my life. So, I really can't abide the narrative when we separate women and men. But of one thing I'm absolutely sure. I have a sacred responsibility and a right to reject and fight against patriarchy in all of its forms. Even within caucus, I have that right and that sacred responsibility. Because if I don't do it, who does it for the next generation? So, when I say I'm a feminist, that's what I mean. I mean I have a sacred responsibility, and I believe all women have this same sacred responsibility, to fight patriarchy whenever it appears.

> " *I have a sacred responsibility, and I believe all women have this same sacred responsibility, to fight patriarchy whenever it appears.*

Creating Enduring Change

In order to create meaningful change, the political system itself must change through electoral reform; governments can introduce analytical tools and democratic reforms — including electoral reform, gender-based analysis plus (GBA+) and gender-responsive budgeting (GRB) — to identify and address unintended bias.

Electoral reform is a necessary aspect of structural change and can be designed to encourage the adoption of a gender-balanced slate of candidates. The current systems, including Canada's plurality ("first past the post"), present challenges to women seeking to be elected because the focus is generally considered to be on the party not the candidate. Efforts to pass electoral reform, where Canada's plurality system would be changed, were dropped by the government in 2016. In the absence of democratic reform in Canada, political parties bear the responsibility of changing the political landscape both through the recruitment and promotion of women in politics and through their platforms.

GBA+ is applicable for policymakers at all levels — municipal, provincial, and federal. The AFN Women's Council also advocates a gender-balanced perspective within First Nations communities. GBA+ training teaches politicians to imagine how decisions on a policy, program, initiative, or service might affect different segments of their constituents and helps legislators to mitigate bias.

Gender-responsive budgeting (GRB) seeks to ensure that budgets benefit the whole of society. The tool addresses the collection and allocation of public resources to ensure that the resources contribute to advancing gender equality and women's empowerment. UN Women supports the development of GRB in over 40 countries.

Creating enduring change means seeing things differently, counting things differently, and putting tools in place institutionally to create change.

CAROLYN BENNETT

Carolyn Bennett has been Toronto-St. Paul's MP since 1997 and has served as the chair of the Liberal Women's Caucus and a minister with several portfolios in cabinet.

The systematic use of gender-based analysis across all government departments is crucial for all policies and budgeting exercises — it is fundamental to evidence-based decision-making. It is something we hoped for since the Beijing Fourth World Conference on Women. It is no longer sufficient to simply send over decisions to the Status of Women to have one department apply the lens. Every department needs to understand the profound nature of this challenge function. Former Minister of Status of Women Patty Hajdu was relentless in insisting all cabinet documents contain gender analysis. In the Senate, Nancy Ruth was a constant champion grilling the generals: "Are you serious about gender or not?"

This is the first federal government with a full ministry whose only job is gender. This is a giant step forward. Even great ministers like Jean Augustine and Hedy Fry had other mandates folded into their portfolio. Minister Maryam Monsef helped support a gender agenda for Canada's G7 presidency and was given wide opportunity to impact change. The prime minister appointed a Gender Equality Advisory Council to provide heads of state input on the G7 Summit.

Women's Caucus is another instrument supporting women members and advancing women through party structures, policies, and platforms. *Pink Books I, II,* and *III,* generated by the Women's Caucus, were the brainchild of Belinda Stronach when she was chair of the caucus and supported by the Liberal Research Bureau. Women's Caucus was a small but mighty group of MPs. We were working coast to coast to recruit remarkable candidates.

JOYCE MURRAY

Joyce Murray was first elected as an MLA for the BC Liberal Party and served as a cabinet minister from 2001 to 2005. She was then elected as an MP for Vancouver Quadra for the Liberal Party in 2008 and was later appointed president of the Treasury Board and Minister of Digital Government.

A s parliamentary secretary to the president of the Treasury Board in Canada's federal government, it was important for me to be well informed on all aspects of the advancement of women's equality and empowerment, a priority of our prime minister [Justin Trudeau]. This includes the application of the gender lens to the budgeting process. Gender-responsive budgeting is an important tool in that toolbox.

UN Women has provided leadership to governments around the world to understand and implement gender-responsive budgeting. In collaboration with other international bodies, like the Commonwealth Secretariat, International Development Research Centre, and the European Commission, UN Women assists policymakers integrate this analysis into their international development plans and measure the allocation of budgets to national policies and programs for the promotion of girls' and women's rights. It also assists foreign policymakers identify targeted budget allocations related to the UN Millennium Development Goals.

Gender-responsive budgeting is an important tool.

" Training and support to women across all parties and around the world is important in politics.

AUDREY MCLAUGHLIN

Audrey McLaughlin was elected as the MP for Yukon for the NDP in and served until 1997. In 1989, she became the first woman to lead a federal party in Canada.

Reaching at least a tipping point of women in Parliament is a very legitimate and important question. I think most people internationally would accept 30 percent as the minimum — a target Canada has not yet reached. Why is it important? We need everybody's perspective. It's why we need First Nations in government. It's why we need people of all Canadian traditions, backgrounds, family structures, and abilities. It brings different perspectives. It is not productive when politics becomes isolated from the day-to-day concerns of the people it represents. It's why you need a mix of rural and urban elected members. Things are very different in urban cities than in rural Canada.

Why 50 percent women? Well, 50 percent of the Canadian population is female. It is not a question of who's better or even who is more qualified. I think the whole thing about qualifications is a bit of a non-sequitur. It is a question of perspective. In Canada, we have a first-past-the-post system. This is not common in electoral systems around the world. Proportional representation provides for greater diversity and gender equity.

One of the most impressive organizations advocating for women in politics is called the 50/50 Group of Sierra Leone. The people of Sierra Leone went through a horrific and cruel civil war. Women came together. They were extremely organized and effective. To get to 50 percent women, they worked exhaustively to put together a list for all parties of talented women who would be good candidates and good cabinet ministers. The easy excuse for overlooking women — "We hunted but could not find any women" — was silenced. In the toughest of circumstances, it was an impressive strategy by women to champion women.

Training and support to women across all parties and around the world is important in politics. Women need to know the rules of their parties, their legislatures, Parliaments, and committees. We need to provide women access to a range of the training options available in Canada and abroad.

KIM CAMPBELL

In 2014, former PC prime minister Kim Campbell proposed the controversial idea of dual-member ridings, where one woman and one man would be elected in every riding, which she said would both encourage more women to enter politics and increase the representation of women in politics.

P olitical process may not be a compelling story for the public press, yet process is integral to whether you succeed or not; where the levers of power reside and how they can be invoked matter. I had a lot of ideas about process. Some of them I didn't get a chance to implement because it was nearing the end of summer, and I had to drop the writ and turn my full attention to the federal election.

I had proposed important changes in the way prime ministerial power works, parliamentary process, cabinet structure, and federal-provincial relations. I was able to act on a few issues of democratic reform. We reconfigured the ministries of government and made the cabinet more streamlined. I convened the first-ever meeting of provincial premiers prior to the G7 summit. Many of the issues of the G7 summit are actually areas of provincial jurisdiction, and I wanted to meet with the provincial premiers to discuss some things that were on the G7 agenda. We held a meeting in Vancouver just before I went to Tokyo.

Process doesn't always make riveting press stories. But I view process as critical to good governance. For example, having led the Peter Lougheed Leadership College at the University of Alberta, I thought a great deal about negotiations to repatriate the Constitution. Governing involves personalities and relationships. It is very important to design mechanisms for bringing people together to find ways around challenging issues.

I had put out a document when I was running for the leadership. I believe I described it in my memoir, *Time and Chance*. The document outlined some of the profound changes I wanted to introduce to government process. For one, I was concerned that backbenchers, who work hard for their constituents to bring diverse voices to Ottawa, often disagree with government positions. While they can argue their positions strongly in caucus, this is not public. I wondered why not. What you stand for is important. I felt the process needed further examination. Strong and transparent process is important in creating public confidence in political branches.

ANDREA HORWATH

Andrea Horwath, leader of the Ontario NDP, MPP, and former Hamilton city councillor, believes electoral reform could help achieve gender parity in government.

We need to look at different democratic reform tools. I think we need to look at the way that we elect people. The NDP has long been on the record for a system of voting called mixed-member proportional representation. It is a system where some people are elected at large by the electorate and others are put in place by the parties based on the number of votes that they received. In this way, there is the opportunity for parties to ensure gender balance and diversity of racial and ethical representation as well as address other intersectional qualities. When you look at democracies in the world which have that kind of system of voting, you see quite a more diverse representation of the population in legislatures.

I think we need to look at the way that we elect people.

MEN AS PARTNERS FOR CHANGE

Many of the women interviewed for *Women on the Ballot* mentioned ways that men had helped support them. People in positions of political power can advance legislation removing systemic gender barriers and addressing gender inequality in society — and can reach out to ensure women in the community are adequately resourced to run as candidates. For example, Prime Minister Justin Trudeau introduced a gender-balanced cabinet in 2015, catapulting Canada to fifth place internationally in terms of the percentage of women in ministerial positions. When Canada assumed presidency of the G7 in 2018, Trudeau created the Gender Equality Advisory Council "to ensure gender equality and the empowerment of women and girls guided all discussions and activities" while Canada was president.

Jack Layton, leader of the federal NDP (2003–2011), recruited, persuaded, equipped, and empowered many women to run for political office. Layton's caucuses contained higher proportions of women relative to other federal parties. In the 2011 federal election, the NDP elected 40 women, the highest number of women ever to serve in the Official Opposition.

Liberal MP Mauril Bélanger, before his death in August 2016, put his private member's Bill C-210 before the House of Commons to change the words in Canada's national anthem to be gender inclusive — changing the second line from "in all thy sons command" to "in all of us command." Also in 2016, NDP MP Kennedy Stewart sponsored a private member's bill in the House to amend the Canada Elections Act. Bill C-237, the Candidate Gender Equity Act, proposed reducing the reimbursement that registered political parties receive for their election expenses if there is greater than a 10 percent difference in the number of male and female candidates on the party's list for a general election.

See the Appendix (page 226) for further examples of legislation that contributes to the advancement of gender equality and women's empowerment.

More Than Just Numbers

What changes when a critical mass of women is elected? Empowering women in politics is more than just increasing numbers: women's presence in politics changes the conversation and culture. Many of the women interviewed for this book discussed the difference in how people speak — the tone and the tenor of conversations — when more women are elected. Others commented on how the decision-making process changes and the diversification of issues increases, which consequently leads to changes in how resources are allocated to the public. Some of these policy changes resonate at the local level, including effective snow removal for those with mobility devices, guide dogs, or strollers; others are significant on the international stage, including peace initiatives that consider how women are used as tools of war. The 2018 G7 Gender Equality Advisory Council found that gender equality is the number one predictor of peace.

VALÉRIE PLANTE

Valérie Plante served one term on Montreal City Council (2013–2017) before her successful bid for the leadership of the Projet Montréal Party (2016) and before being elected the mayor of Montreal in 2017. When Plante became mayor, she upset incumbent and former federal minister Denis Coderre.

I became the first women in the 375-year history of the city to occupy this privileged position.

E lected as mayor of Montreal in November 2017, I became the first woman in the 375-year history of the city to occupy this privileged position. It has given to me the remarkable chance to implement an ambitious and focused agenda. Our campaign was values-driven. I want to see those values translated into the structures and spaces of governance. A part of this vision was the appointment of a gender-balanced executive committee — including members of the Opposition. When Montreal elected its first Indigenous councillor, I asked her to be a part of this executive committee. First Nations have been on this land for thousands of years. Their voice is vital to our deliberations and a part of building a vibrant and sustainable future.

ANDREA HORWATH

Elected leader of the Ontario NDP in 2009, Andrea Horwath became the first woman to lead the Ontario NDP.

It made a significant difference when the caucus was 50 percent women. The tone changed. Priorities changed. It also changed the process of decision-making around the table. It was absolutely enriching not only for the women but for the men as well. Before we had a 50 percent female caucus, decisions were very quickly taken. People took a side. If someone was bringing something forward, people around the table would observe who was supporting that particular idea, and then everything would shake down quickly from there. Nowadays, it is completely different. There seems to be a much greater amount of discussion and dialogue. There is less often a quick jump to take decisions based on who it is that happens to be talking. The process is just better. The exchange is more respectful and more engaging. It pulls people into a collective decision-making process. It is not always consensus — we don't always reach consensus — but we certainly come to conclusions in a much more open way. It is also my view that when women bring their life experiences and diverse perspectives to the discussion, it changes the policies being discussed and the priority that different issues have at the table.

It made a significant difference when the caucus was 50 percent women. The tone changed. Priorities changed.

JOANNE BERNARD

In 2013, Joanne Bernard was elected as the MLA for Dartmouth North for the Nova Scotia Liberal Party. She had many roles in the government, including the Minister of Community Services and the Minister responsible for the Disabled Persons' Commission Act.

The impact was more than just the number and visibility of women in politics. The conversation and the culture changed.

Having female voices around a cabinet table changes the cadence of the conversation. Women at the decision table change the culture of work. When we came into power, I think we tripled the number of women MLAs in Nova Scotia. Women were also put into critical roles by the premier. The impact was more than just the number and visibility of women in politics. The conversation and the culture changed. Women, when they are present in significant numbers, bring a sense of respectful listening and careful conversation.

LINDA SLAVIN

Linda Slavin ran for the NDP in Peterborough, Ontario, at all three levels of government. Slavin was on the organizing committee for Peterborough's Leap Manifesto in 2015, a call to action against climate change.

I believe increased numbers of women in politics are essential to addressing the urgency of peace, human security, and climate change action.

I believe increased numbers of women in politics are essential to addressing the urgency of peace, human security, and climate change action. Greta Thunberg, the Swedish teen leading international action on the climate crisis, insists that politicians must listen to scientists and act now to meet their international obligations. It is a strong call from a young woman who is inspiring a generation of youth to demand change.

Politicians need to know the limited time frame for action — 11 years to make drastic reductions in carbon emissions by 2030. We need to involve the world's best minds in finding solutions — and

50 percent of those best minds belong to women. This is perhaps the best argument for gender parity in politics and elsewhere. [Skills that women have] are extremely important to have represented in our political system. Women traditionally are marginalized in the political system, as they are marginalized in life. It is women's stories of learning, caring, and connecting across economic and cultural diversity that we need in order to produce the change that helps all people.

When you get women at the table, the nature of the discussion changes.

KATHLEEN WYNNE

When Kathleen Wynne was Liberal premier of Ontario, she wrote an open letter to Canadian women in *The Kit*, calling for more women to run, saying that "when women become a critical mass at the table — whether it's in the boardroom or in cabinet or in corner offices — that's when the real change happens."

When you get women at the table, the nature of the discussion changes. Having women at the decision table in a political context inevitably leads to different issues being discussed. In my experience, priority is placed on issues around children, education, housing, and healthcare. During my time as premier, we made decisions, such as the one to put more money into the salaries of personal support workers, which impacted largely on women's lives. We wanted to ensure that increased support to male-dominated sectors like firefighting was matched by equivalent increases in sectors where women dominated.

When there was all the publicity around the Jian Ghomeshi public assault incidences in public broadcasting, I saw this as an opportunity to implement some changes for women in the workplaces and at their places of study. For example, we mandated sexual assault policies on all campuses and that students be involved in creating those policies. I had many people tell me that would not have happened if women were not leading the charge.

ALEXA MCDONOUGH

Elected leader of the Nova Scotia NDP in 1980, Alexa McDonough was one of the first women to lead a provincial party, and when she first gained a seat in 1981, she was the sole NDP member of the legislature. McDonough served in the provincial legislature from 1981 to 1995, as federal leader of the NDP from 1995 to 2003, and MP from 1997 to 2008.

Equity would imply that people at the decision-making table reflect the population they represent. Having been at the early stages of the battle for women in politics, I can controversially say that even one woman can be a tipping point of sorts. Even the presence of one woman who is willing to stand up and speak out about the culture at the decision-making table and the issues being debated can disrupt the flow.

If you get even three women, you can begin to build a sisterhood. Supporting this sisterhood and their success also depends on your ability to draw other women into the movement so that they're activists at the constituency level, at the provincial level, and in the party organization. Hitting the tipping point, or critical point, has to go beyond the legislature and into the structure and local executives and campaigns. I think of it as almost spreading horizontally just as much as advancing vertically in terms of elected women.

Equity would imply that people at the decision-making table reflect the population they represent.

EVA AARIAK

An Inuit leader, Eva Aariak grew up in Arctic Bay on Baffin Island in Nunavut and in 2008 became the first woman premier of Nunavut.

I was the first female premier of the territory and the fifth female premier in Canada. At my first Council of the Federation meeting, a meeting of the premiers of each of Canada's 13 provinces and territories, I was just absorbing everything. I was the only woman among the premiers. When other women premiers were elected and [joined] subsequent councils, I could feel the difference in culture. We were always respected, but when the gender balance changed, I heard more discussion on social issues and community perspectives. I sensed that when other women premiers came on board, things changed in these subtle ways.

When the gender balance changed, I heard more discussion on social issues and community perspectives.

> **"**
> *Women look at issues differently. Women set priorities differently than men.*

DEB MATTHEWS

Deb Matthews served as MPP from 2003 to 2018 for London North Centre in Ontario, with subsequent cabinet posts as Minister of Health and Long-Term Care, Minister of Children and Youth Services, and Deputy Premier, among others, for the Ontario Liberal Party.

I cannot stress enough how important it is that the voice of all the people is heard in the legislature, in the cabinet room, and in caucus. Gender is a big part of that equation. Women look at issues differently. Women set priorities differently than men. No question about it. In 2003, when I was elected, there was a whole crop of new Liberals elected. Many of us were women, and we formed a women's caucus. First, we decided that we were not going to be the pink-collar ghetto caucus. We wanted to deal with issues that mattered most to women, including child poverty. Some of the issues we identified seemed to have been overlooked because not enough of us had been involved in the dialogue. The women's caucus helped sharpen our focus on issues disproportionately impacting the lives of women and children.

JEANNETTE MONTUFAR

People of all genders can be successful advocates of equity and equality or can harbour prejudices. Jeannette Montufar, PC provincial candidate in the 2016 Manitoba election, argues that reaching the tipping point is more than just numbers.

Discussing the term tipping point is complex because it's not only about numbers; it's about the quality of the people at the table. Governing bodies should have at least 50 percent women, but women can be as gender-blind as men — and men can be very gender-progressive. The quality of representation of women and men matters. If we seek to bring diversity and inclusion to debates, we have to acknowledge that quality matters too. Numbers can achieve gender balance, but achieving a tipping point in debates means electing women and men aware of women's issues and committed to gender mainstreaming to achieve equality in Canada.

Governing bodies should have at least 50 percent women, but women can be as gender-blind as men — and men can be very gender-progressive.

> **"**
> *The world view would be different with women in politics.*

OLIVIA CHOW

Olivia Chow was elected school trustee in 1985 and served on the Toronto Board of Education until 1991, when she was elected city councillor. Chow was the first Asian-born woman elected to Toronto City Council and served until 2005. Elected as an MP in 2006 for the NDP, she won re-election twice. In 2015, she joined Ryerson University as a Distinguished Visiting Professor.

I have one piece of advice for women — the only one: Be very clear what you want to change and why you want to do it. If you are going into politics because there is something that you think is unfair, something that could be improved, a policy change or budget change to accomplish something — then go for it. You need to be passionate about what you want to change.

Some goals can take decades of activism, not always inside politics. Alexa McDonough, in the wake of the 9/11 attacks in 2001, led the successful cause to repatriate Maher Arar. In my case, I was at the forefront of the campaign to achieve a national apology and redress for the discriminatory Chinese head tax. It took from 1983 until 2006. You do not necessarily have to be in power to achieve goals if you are clear and relentless on what you want to do.

If you look at our society today, you will notice that a lot of services for children and seniors — people who need more nurturing or who are sick — are mostly provided by women. Personal care workers and childcare workers are underpaid partially because we have governments that do not see these services as a government responsibility. Protective services are seen as a state responsibility, whereas childcare, early childhood education, and taking care of seniors are seen as a family responsibility. That is a world view I do not share. I think women's world view of what is a government responsibility is different. Men tend to see protective services — police and military — as essential. No one would debate those as government responsibilties. But childcare and early childhood education are not. I believe the world view would be different with women in politics. Secondly, I believe politics would have a more collaborative approach with more women being elected at different levels of government.

KAREN MCCRIMMON

As Canada's first woman air navigator and the first woman to command an air force squadron, Karen McCrimmon worked in the male-dominated armed forces before running for office for the Liberal Party. She was elected as an MP in 2015 for Kanata-Carleton in Ontario.

Once you have a critical number of women around the table, people aren't afraid to ask questions anymore.

I think the style of communication changes when more women are at the decision table. I think the collaborative nature changes a little bit. Mixed decision tables get more perspectives. I observe that more questions are asked. That's what I've seen. Once you have a critical number of women around the table, people aren't afraid to ask questions anymore. When a room is male-dominated, I think people feel more constrained, and a hierarchy sets in. Women seem to engender a more open and free exploration of issues and ask more frank and open questions. Women, and I number among them, when they feel they should know something but don't have the information at hand, seem more inclined to ask another woman to get at critical information and move on solutions.

FLORA MACDONALD

The late Flora MacDonald was a treasured friend. We discussed this book on several occasions. Hanging on her den wall and peering down on our conversations was a picture of the 107 members of the 1972 Progressive Conservative Party caucus. She was the only woman. Flora had few female models in politics as her point of reference. She broke the mould becoming the first woman to be Minister of External Affairs in Canada and the first woman to compete for the leadership of a major political party in 1976. She began her journey as secretary in the national office of the *Progressive* Conservative Party (she always placed an emphasis on that first word).

In her bid to win the party leadership in 1976, many committed delegates who had promised to cast their "Flora vote" did not do so behind the black curtains of the ballot box. In a dramatic turn of events, first-round ballots were tabulated, and Flora's predicted strong standing vanished. Later during the leadership convention, she decided to back MP Joe Clark. He won. Flora went into cabinet. Perhaps the leadership race reflected some discomfort with women's leadership. It certainly taught the lesson that delivering your committed supporters to the ballot box may not translate into votes. The "Flora Syndrome" is a caution to candidates to this day.

When we spoke, as we almost always did, of women's representation in Parliament, Flora labelled women's progress as glacial. I called her an impatient feminist, although I am not sure she agreed with the term.

Shortly before her death, I asked her this question: "If you had only one thing to say to the next wave of women considering politics, what would it be?"

She replied swiftly and characteristically to the point.

"Never doubt yourself."

THAT'S IT!
I'M RUNNING!

In 2008, in the JFK Jr. Forum at Harvard Kennedy School, the air was electric. It was the night when the Barack Obama campaign "Yes, We Can" — did! Blue, red, and white balloons sailed down from the ceiling flooding the floor of the Forum as the first African American person in history won the presidency.

The air was thick with exuberance and expectation. The lucky ones who had won tickets to the Institute of Politics "Election Night Celebration" were high on hope.

It was different that night in 2016.

The balloons were again suspended from the ceiling. Electoral results poured onto the big screen. The boisterous crowd grew increasingly hushed as CNN anchors reported the returns in rapid fire. Those of us who had been in Beijing at the 1995 Fourth UN Conference on Women, when Hillary Clinton addressed 40 000 women from around the world with the words "women's rights are human rights," felt the sting of what was happening.

A different reality was taking hold. The results hung in the balance for some time that night before the new president was announced. The balloons were still suspended when I left.

The next morning, at the Harvard Kennedy School Women and Public Policy Program (WAPPP) in Cambridge, Massachusetts, a small group of us watched as Clinton delivered her concession speech. There had been a lot of hopes riding on this one. The United States had had the possibility of electing an intelligent, articulate, experienced woman with a long track record of championing girls and women globally. It was a dream too good to be true. As with any candidate, there were faults to be found. But Clinton's potential could not be denied.

In the end, it was. I felt sad, angry, abandoned, betrayed, and exasperated all at once. The "best man for the job" had been a woman. What had happened? Many hearts sank as Clinton's words trailed away.

Then a strange thing started happening.

The cellphone of Victoria Budson, WAPPP's Executive Director, lit up with a string of incoming calls. My BlackBerry also started buzzing with text messages from women across Canada. The words were the same on both phones. A series of short static statements:

"That's it! I'm running!"

It was like oxygen.

ACKNOWLEDGEMENTS

First and foremost, recognition goes to the remarkable trailblazers in this book, who generously gave their stories to empower future generations of women in politics.

This book would not have been written without the leadership of people from my three campaigns: Vicky Martins and Mary MacPherson, friends and co-chairs of my first federal campaign; Jon Grant and the late Erica Cherney, who convened the community Advisory Council; Dr. Kelly Butler, a lifelong friend; invaluable supporters Lynne Steele, Alexis Levine, and Tom Allison; co-chairs Ted Murray and Elaine Tracey, chair Andy Mitchell, and countless campaign volunteers.

During the time I was a fellow with David Gergen at the Harvard Kennedy School (HKS) and a member of the Harvard Women's Leadership Board, several HKS colleagues inspired my path in public service and politics, including Holly Taylor Sargent, Sheila Jasanoff, Hannah Riley Bowles, Barbara Kellerman, Iris Bohnet, Ambassador Swanee Hunt, the late Calestous Juma, Victoria Budson, and Kerri Collins. Kim Campbell, whom I met at the Harvard Kennedy School, ignited my drive to record the path of Canadian women in politics.

Lakefield author John Boyko and Montreal author Guy Stanley gave in-depth time and imagination to my journey writing this book. Rosemary Ganley, Ann Douglas, and I shared lively conversations and analytical commentary.

Thirty student volunteers across Canada on three youth teams were at the heart of the book. Six co-chairs — Edward Tian, Sneha Wadhwani, Shelby Hayes, Thomas Kaplanniak, Charlotte McParland, and Mitchell Fox — coordinated the teams. David de Paiva led legislative research. Members of the youth team were Alina Asghar, Graeme Cannon, Ruth Chen, Chloe Cheung, Kitty Cheung, Elaina Anne Cox, Joseph Garcelon, Nick Harris, Anne-Eloïse Hay, Audrey Ho, Anthony Lenarduzzi, Jimmy Li, Ryan Newman, Marium Nur Vahed, Ashley Persaud, Katherine Petrasek, Jordan Porter, Sarah Rana, Hannah Ruuth, Kate Schneider, Alanna Sokic, Kordell Walsh, and Keren Wemegah.

Heather Watson was the backbone of project management and Cammie Jaquays, a solid support. Women of excellence in other disciplines, Sharon Woods (mountaineer), Roberta Bondar (astronaut), and Nicole Cooke (cyclist) are friends I interviewed exploring insights from their fields applicable to women in politics.

Terry McQuitty offered valuable observations. Steve Paikin gave insights on the goals of the book. Andrew Cardoso,

president of the Pearson Centre, hosted a book preview. Nancy Peckford and her colleagues at Equal Voice and all the women in campaign schools never doubted this was an important undertaking.

I would also like to thank Rubicon Publishing, including associate publisher Amy Land, editors Terri Carleton and Stephanie Rotz, and publisher Maggie Goh.

My family were my foundation and compass. I could not have done what I did without them. My thanks to Barb, John and Robert and Gail, Marg and Ross, Kaleigh and Kristy, my son, Mac, and Diane and their daughters, Mae and Lauren. Thanks especially to my nephew Robert, finishing his own book, *Journey of 1,000 Steps*. We shared the remarkable journey of an author.

ARE YOU READY TO BE A CANDIDATE?

A Potential Candidate's Decision Path and Campaign Timeline

By Harry Mortimer MBA, CPA, CMA

A potential candidate for any contest has to make a significant commitment to being a candidate. Often there is limited information to help make an informed and final decision. Typically, potential contestants will enter the pre-contest period and test the waters. The following timeline shows the campaign activities, critical assessment criteria, and the common exit points that are taken by a potential candidate on the path to an election.

The road to follow for a candidate is a long one. The commitment may take years to fulfil. The 30 to 60 days of an election that the electors see is only a short period on the timeline for the candidate. Many campaigns include a two-step process, which includes both a nomination campaign and an election campaign. Once the vote is over, there is also the statutory reporting that can linger for years. Of course if you win, your commitment may lead to years in public office.

REVIEW AND ASSESSMENT:
Are you ready to be a candidate?

Potential candidates need to self-assess if they want to make a commitment to run for public office. This assessment may take minutes to years. Use all of the time available to you, and understand what you are getting into before you make your decision. Do not be shy to discuss questions with your family and with those who have taken the electoral path before you. Questions to consider:

- Are you ready for a commitment to public life?
- What are the consequences to your career or business?
- How will your decision impact others? Can you gain experience by actively volunteering in campaigns for others? Have you been recruited by others to act as a candidate?
- Do your skills and interests match the position you want to run for?

PRE-CONTEST PERIOD:
Undeclared candidate preparing for a campaign

The pre-contest period gives potential candidates a chance to assess and develop their skills and to build a support team. This is a low-risk period where you can test the waters for support and determine your own comfort with public life. Some potential candidates will learn that it is best not to run, and others will gain confidence that they are strong, viable candidates. The earlier that you engage, the more opportunity there is to strengthen your campaign. Pre-contest activities include the following:

1. Shameless self-promotion
- Develop a social media presence — let people know your interests and let them get to know you.
- Develop a media presence — does the media see you as a viable contributor?
- Engage with the community — take a leadership role in an area of your personal interest. Join a charity or interest group.

2. Build your networks
- Participate in community events — volunteer, seek profile positions, such as the MC for local events.
- Be active in partisan activities — show others your interest. Take on fundraising and organizational challenges to develop and show your skills to others.

3. Reality check
Test the waters for support — ask others what it would take to support you if you proceed.

4. Build a campaign plan
Lay out the strategic and financial plans necessary for a successful campaign. A plan needs to be flexible to suit different levels of fundraising and responsive to meet strategic priorities. If you cannot put a plan on paper, how can you expect to successfully run a campaign?

TEST THE WATERS

5. Recruit a campaign team

To start, build a team from your closest friends — individuals who are willing to make a commitment to support you in whatever way is possible. Assign temporary roles to the earliest volunteers, and continue to recruit more experienced volunteers to fill the positions with specific skills.

• Find a campaign manager

You will likely have different managers as you proceed through different stages of the campaign. Early in the pre-contest period, you will need someone to focus on keeping things organized and developing volunteer engagement. As you proceed into an active campaign, you will need a more experienced manager with a solid understanding of strategic implementation for the campaign.

• Find an official/financial agent

This will likely be the longest-serving volunteer on your campaign. This is the senior management role for the campaign. Ensure that you recruit a committed personal friend that you can rely on to protect your interests. Experience with accounting and record-keeping is a beneficial asset for an agent but should not be your first or only criterion. Finance and accounting are only a part of the job, so you can recruit other volunteers to assist the agent with that part of the job.

• Build a volunteer base

A campaign needs to recruit many volunteers for many different tasks. Some volunteers will commit more time and energy than others, but every volunteer is valuable. Volunteers disappear quickly if they do not find rewarding tasks to keep them busy when they are called on to help. Ensure that you can assign tasks to keep volunteers engaged. At this early stage, ask for small time commitments with specific jobs. Build an inventory list of volunteer interests and training opportunities.

6. Seek a nomination

Different contests will have very different nomination requirements. This may simply be a self-nomination, or you may be required to compete in a nomination contest on its own.

7. Pre-election/Pre-contest campaign engagement

Take advantage of the pre-contest period for more than just planning. Treat it as an extended campaign period. Use the time to identify your vote, build your organization, and define yourself as a candidate.

• Define the candidate

This is a period of shameless self-promotion. Seek as many opportunities as possible to present yourself as a potential candidate to the community. Seek as much media exposure as you can (where possible).

• Voter identification

Early identification helps define campaign strategy and reduces costs during the election period.

• Campaign planning

Identify areas of strength and areas that need reinforcement. Assess the resources required to gain support for the campaign.

• Connect with circles of influence

Build relationships with community leaders and community interest groups.

ELECTION PERIOD:
Declared as a candidate

Every election will have a formal start date and end at the close of the polls. Campaigns vary from 30 to 90 days. At the call of the contest, you will need to declare as a candidate. Check in advance the legal requirements specific to your contest. The common actions required include the following:

1. Candidate registration/nomination

There will be a paperwork process identifying the candidate. Often this will require signatures of eligible electors as a nomination.

2. Appoint an auditor

Identify an eligible auditor for your campaign. Ensure that the auditor has past experience with the same type of campaign reporting and that he or she can provide advisory services throughout the campaign.

3. Open a bank account

A separate bank account is normally required for maintaining campaign transactions.

4. Fundraising

The greatest number of contributions can be collected during the election period. Supporters can see the need to fund a campaign and are willing to contribute. Generally contribution limits apply.

5. Campaign activities

There are endless activities for a campaign to undertake. The common priorities include the following:

- Continued voter identification
- Persuasion — reinforce the candidate, policy support, ethics, interests
- Fundraising
- Recruit/engage volunteers
- Get out the vote — GOTV

6. Candidate activities

These activities will keep the candidate busy night and day:

- Outreach to the voters, including door knocking, speeches, fundraising, meet-and-greets, and media interviews
- Provide leadership for the campaign volunteers
- Active learning, reading and research of voters' issues
- Daily updates of campaign policies
- Review and agreement with campaign marketing materials

7. Election day

The popularity of advance voting has now extended election day to many days or weeks. In any case, the goal is all about getting out the vote. This is the time when you rely on the most volunteers, and it can be one of the most expensive days for a campaign. You will need to feed and transport both volunteers and voters. You also need space for volunteers to gather and organize.

THE GOAL

POST-ELECTION REPORTING PERIOD

Four main jobs remain after the election:

1. Reporting

Once the election is over, win or lose, there are statutory reporting requirements. Typically all of the volunteers have disappeared, and the campaign manager will move on to new challenges. The financial agent has to pull together the finances and complete the reporting. If there is debt, the problems become more complex. There is a three-to-four-month period to prepare for financial reporting, get all the bills paid, and prepare for an audit.

2. Audit

Most statutory reporting requirements will require an audit of the financial reporting if transactions exceed a minimum threshold. Do not underestimate the time that the auditor will require to conduct an audit. This will typically be a minimum of 30 to 60 days. Confirm with your auditor the time required to conduct the audit.

3. Post-audit statuatory review

Once the audit is complete and everything is filed, there is typically a statutory review; it may take months or years to finalize a campaign return. You will need to sit back and wait for the review to be completed. The review can identify new problems for the campaign to deal with, or it can confirm that everything is complete. Typically the campaign bank account remains open through this period.

4. Final responsibilities

One of the last activities will be for the campaign to close the bank account and report any campaign surplus. This is when the responsibilities of the candidate and the financial agent come to an end.

This information has been prepared for general discussion purposes only and should not be viewed as interpretation of any statutory requirements or contest rules.

CAMPAIGN CLEAN-UP

EXIT

ROAD TO NEXT ELECTION

WHAT DOES IT TAKE: SELECTED ORGANIZATIONS AND INITIATIVES

Assembly of First Nations (AFN) Women's Council	The Women's Council works with the AFN Secretariat to hold a "wide range of activities and initiatives relevant to First Nations women," including an Indigenous Women's Summit.
Canadian Labour Congress (CLC): Candidate Development for Women	The CLC runs a course designed to address the challenges that women candidates face at the municipal, provincial, and/or federal levels — including campaign strategies, presentation skills, etc.
Democracy Kit	The Democracy Project and Democracy Kit provide designed campaign kits, community directories, online training webinars, and events to encourage engagement in local politics.
Elections Canada: Inspire Democracy	Elections Canada provides a step-by-step guide to running in a federal election (thinking about being a candidate, becoming a candidate, being a candidate, and reporting).
Equal Voice & Daughters of the Vote	Equal Voice is a bilingual and multipartisan organization dedicated to electing more women to all levels of political office in Canada. "Daughters of the Vote" is a banner initiative that brings 338 young women to Parliament Hill for a session to occupy 100% of the seats in the House of Commons.
Federation of Canadian Municipalities (FCM): Women in Local Government	FCM offers online and in-person training for women running for municipal government, including the toolkit "Diverse Voices: Tools and Practices to Support all Women."
G(irls)20	G(irls)20 has two programs: the Global Summit and Girls on Boards. Girls on Boards trains and places young women on non-profit governance boards in their communities across Canada. The G(irls)20 Summit invests in international delegates to economically empower girls and women in their home country.

Girls in Politics (GIP) Initiative	GIP programs introduce girls and young women aged 8 to 17 to politics, policy, the work of the United States Congress, parliamentary governments, and the work of the United Nations.
The Institute for Change Leaders	The Institute for Change Leaders hosts different training and workshops that teach "the skills that organizers need to win social change," including how to tell your story, recruit volunteers, structure a team, fundraise, and more.
International Knowledge Network of Women in Politics: iKNOW Politics	iKNOW Politics is an online forum and resource centre that aims to increase women's participation in politics.
Legislative Assembly of Ontario: Model Parliament for High School and Post-Secondary Students	The Legislative Assembly of Ontario hosts model parliaments for high school and post-secondary students to learn about and participate in democracy. Applications are accepted in the fall.
Queen's Female Leadership in Politics (QFLIP)	QFLIP is a three-day undergraduate conference to empower students from across Canada to engage in politics.
St. Francis Xavier University: Indigenous Women in Community Leadership	Indigenous Women in Community Leadership is a fully funded scholarship program "for First Nations, Métis and Inuit women who are committed to supporting development and social change in their organizations, communities and Nations."
Women Win Toronto	Women Win Toronto trains and prepares women from diverse backgrounds to run winning municipal campaigns.
YWCA: Think Big! Lead Now! Young Women's National Leadership Program	This bilingual leadership program has online learning sessions, talks, self-study, peer mentorship, and civic engagement activities, along with a three-day immersive training and networking summit.

A WORLD MADE ANEW: SELECTED LEGISLATION

BILL	INTENT	PASSED
Canada-Wide		
Bill S-207: Boards of Directors Modernization Act *Introduced by Céline Hervieux-Payette*	A bill to modernize the composition of the boards of directors of certain corporations, financial institutions, and parent Crown corporations to ensure the balanced representation of women and men on those boards.	NO
Bill C-16: An Act to Amend the Canadian Human Rights Act and the Criminal Code *Introduced by Jody Wilson-Raybould*	A bill to change the Canadian Human Rights Act to add gender identity/ expression to the list of prohibited grounds of discrimination. It also allows for gender identity/expression to count as the basis for a hate crime.	YES
Bill C-237: Candidate Gender Equity Act *Introduced by Kennedy Stewart*	A bill to reduce the reimbursement federal political parties receive under the Canada Elections Act if their slate of candidates features a more than 10% disparity between male and female candidates.	NO
Bill C-210: An Act to Amend the National Anthem Act *Introduced by Mauril Bélanger*	A bill to eliminate gender references from the Canadian national anthem, thereby making it gender-neutral.	YES
Motion M-103: A Motion to Condemn Systemic Racism and Religious Discrimination *Introduced by Iqra Khalid*	A motion to condemn and recognize systemic racism and religious discrimination in all its forms and to conduct research for a national action plan.	YES

Bill C-337: An Act to Amend the Judges Act and the Criminal Code (Sexual Assault) *Introduced by Rona Ambrose*	A bill to require that potential judges complete training to dispel myths and falsehoods around the subject of sexual assault, as well as amend the Criminal Code to require statements of explanation in every case surrounding sexual assault.	YES
Bill S-215: An Act to Amend the Criminal Code (Sentencing for Violent Offences Against Aboriginal Women) *Introduced by Senator Lillian Eva Dyck*	A bill to amend the Criminal Code of Canada to consider a woman's Aboriginal status as an aggravating circumstance when imposing a sentence for a violent crime.	YES
Bill C-65: An Act to Amend the Canada Labour Code, the Parliamentary Employment and Staff Relations Act and the Budget Implementation Act, 2017 *Introduced by Patty Hajdu*	This bill strengthens measures to counteract sexual violence and harassment in the workplace.	YES
Ontario		
Bill 68: Modernizing Ontario's Municipal Legislation Act, 2017 *Introduced by Bill Mauro*	One section of this bill, subsection 228, adds a provision that protects new parents who serve on a municipal council and school boards: they are now permitted to take up to 20 weeks off on parental leave to care for their new child and not have their seat declared as vacant.	YES
Bill 26: Domestic and Sexual Violence Workplace Leave, Accommodation and Training Act, 2016 *Introduced by Peggy Sattler*	A bill to amend the Ontario Employment Standards Act to allow for employees to take a leave of absence of up to 10 days of paid leave if they or their child has experienced domestic or sexual violence.	NO

Bill 77: Affirming Sexual Orientation and Gender Identity Act, 2015 *Introduced by Cheri DiNovo*	A bill to make it illegal to provide treatments with the stated goal of changing a patient's gender identity or sexual orientation.	YES
Bill 96: Anti-Human Trafficking Act, 2017 *Introduced by Indira Naidoo-Harris*	This bill makes it possible for a person to apply for a restraining order on the basis of human trafficking or suspected human trafficking.	YES

Quebec

Bill 27: An Act Respecting the Optimization of Subsidized Educational Childcare Services *Introduced by Francine Charbonneau*	This bill would induce every daycare provider in the province of Quebec to ensure their services conform the government's subsidized plan.	NO
Bill 596: An Act to Amend the Civil Code to Make Judicial Remedies for Victims of Sexual Aggression Imprescriptible *Introduced by Simon Jolin-Barrette*	This bill would mandate that victims of sexual harassment and assault would have no limit on how much time can pass between the incident and their filing a suit against their aggressor.	NO
Bill 595: An Act to Protect Access to Institutions Where Elective Abortions Are Performed *Introduced by Carole Poirier*	This bill would mandate that all centres where abortions are performed be surrounded by a no protest zone around the clinics.	NO
Bill 1190: An Act to Establish Gender-Balanced Representation Among Cabinet Ministers *Introduced by Manon Massé*	This bill would mandate that at least 50% of all Quebec provincial cabinets be composed of women.	NO

Bill 151: An Act to Prevent and Fight Sexual Violence in Higher Education Institutions *Introduced by Hélène David*	This bill mandates that all higher education institutions must craft a sexual violence prevention and punishment policy by 2019.	YES
British Columbia		
Bill M 218: Poverty Reduction and Economic Inclusion Act, 2016 *Introduced by Michelle Mungall*	Calls for the development and implementation of a poverty reduction strategy to increase equality and economic inclusion.	NO
Alberta		
Bill 2: An Act to Remove Barriers for Survivors of Sexual and Domestic Violence *Introduced by Kathleen Ganley*	A bill to remove the limitation period in reporting sexual assault or battery.	YES
Bill 202: Protecting Victims of Non-Consensual Distribution of Intimate Images Act *Introduced by Scott Cyr*	A bill that gives school boards the authority to suspend or expel students who violate another student's privacy by spreading intimate images of them without their consent and for victims to seek remuneration for the damages.	YES
Saskatchewan		
Bill 604: An Act to Provide Support for Victims of Domestic Violence *Introduced by Nicole Sarauer*	A bill to mandate employers to provide paid leave and accommodations to employees who are victims of domestic violence.	NO

Manitoba

Bill 221: The Missing and Murdered Indigenous Women and Girls Awareness Day Act *Introduced by Nahanni Fontaine*	This bill would make October 4th known as Missing and Murdered Indigenous Women and Girls Honouring and Awareness Day in Manitoba.	YES
Bill 3: The Post-Secondary Sexual Violence and Sexual Harassment Policies Act *Introduced by James Allum*	A bill to ensure that post-secondary educational institutions have in place policies to counter sexual violence and sexual harassment.	NO
Bill 8: The Employment Standards Code Amendment Act *Introduced by Erna Braun*	A bill to allow employees who suffer from domestic violence to take up to 10 days of leave, as well as a continuous leave period of up to 17 weeks, up to 5 of which must be paid.	YES
Bill 11: The Domestic Violence and Stalking Amendment Act *Introduced by Gord Mackintosh*	A bill to enable a victim of domestic violence or stalking to take out a protection order against the aggressor; also expands the definition of stalking to offences committed over the Internet.	NO
Bill 38: The Intimate Image Protection Act *Introduced by Gord Mackintosh*	A bill to provide victims of non-consensual intimate image distribution with government support; it also establishes the legal framework for victims to sue their aggressors.	YES

New Brunswick

Bill 47: Intimate Partner Violence Intervention Act *Introduced by Brian Gallant*	A bill to allow victims or friends of victims of "intimate partner violence" to apply for an Emergency Intervention Order, which would authorize an authority to intervene in the relationship.	YES

Bill 51: An Act to Amend the Human Rights Act *Introduced by Donald Arsenault*	A bill to amend the New Brunswick Human Rights Act to add family status, sexual orientation, sex, gender identity and expression as prohibited grounds for discrimination.	YES
Nova Scotia		
Bill 29: Pregnancy and Infant Loss Awareness Act *Introduced by Tim Houston*	A bill to ask the Ministry of Health to assess the services available to women and families who experience the loss of a pregnancy or the death of an infant.	NO
Bill 26: Respectful Workplace Week Act *Introduced by Chris d'Entremont*	A bill to make the week beginning on the first Sunday of November known as "Respectful Workplace Week" to encourage a reduction in harassment in workplaces around the province.	NO
Prince Edward Island		
Bill 110: Mandatory Sexual Assault Law Education Act *Introduced by Jamie Fox*	A bill to mandate that all judges receive "education in sexual assault law" before they are allowed to serve in provincial courts.	YES
Bill 25: An Act to amend the Human Rights Act, 2010 *Introduced by Darin King*	A bill to amend the Human Rights Act, 2010 by adding the words "gender identity" and "gender expression" to the list of prohibited grounds of discrimination.	YES
Newfoundland and Labrador		
Bill 43: Access to Abortion Services Act *Introduced by Andrew Parsons*	An act to create safe access zones around facilities and homes of doctors and service providers providing or facilitating abortion services	YES
Bill 25: An Act to Amend the Human Rights Act, 2010 *Introduced by Darin King*	A bill to amend the Human Rights Act, 2010 by adding the words "gender identity" and "gender expression" to the list of prohibited grounds of discrimination	YES

Yukon

Bill 5: An Act to Amend the Human Rights Act and the Vital Statistics Act (2017) *Introduced by Pauline Frost*	A bill to amend the Human Rights Act to add the words "gender identity" and "gender expression" to the list of prohibited grounds of discrimination and amend the Vital Statistics Act to allow a person's sex to be recorded as something other than male or female and allow a person to retroactively change their sex on their birth certificate.	YES
Bill 17: Gender Diversity and Related Amendments Act *Introduced by Jeanie Dendys*	A bill to ensure that government boards and agencies consider the gender and cultural balance in their makeup, while also strengthening measures against discrimination and harassment.	YES

Northwest Territories

Bill 13: The Marriage Act *Introduced by Glen Abernethy*	A bill stating that a person is unable to marry unless the person can be seen to be freely consenting to the marriage by a marriage official.	YES

Nunavut

Bill 6: Official Languages Act *Introduced by Louis Tapardjuk*	The Official Languages Act (OLA) recognizes three official languages in Nunavut: English, French, and Inuit languages.	YES
Bill 7: Inuit Language Protection Act *Introduced by Louis Tapardjuk*	This act aims to increase and protect the population of Inuit who can speak and read their language fluently.	YES

GLOSSARY

Assembly of First Nations (AFN): a national advocacy organization representing First Nations communities in Canada.

Band Council: Under the Indian Act, a Band Council or First Nation council is the band's governing body.

bill: A proposed law submitted to government to be debated upon for approval. A bill can amend or repeal an existing law or propose a new law. There are two kinds of bills: private bills and public bills. Private bills allow a particular person or group of persons an exemption from the general law, while public bills deal with a matter of public policy for the benefit of the community at large and are introduced directly by a member of the House. Private bills should not be confused with private members' bills, which refer to public bills dealing with a matter of public policy introduced by members who are not ministers.

by-election: an election (national, provincial, or municipal) held in a single electoral district outside the schedule of general elections in order to fill a vacancy, usually when a politician dies in office or resigns.

cabinet: the body of advisers that sets the government's policies and priorities for different departments, either for the country or province. Cabinets are chaired by the prime minister or premier; cabinet ministers are most often elected politicians drawn from the party holding the most seats in the House of Commons or legislature.

Canadian Charter of Rights and Freedoms: The Canadian Charter of Rights and Freedoms was enacted in 1982 as a part of the Canadian Constitution. The Charter protects and describes the basic civil rights of all people living in Canada; all laws signed into law must respect these rights.

candidate: a person whose nomination as a candidate in an election has been confirmed and who is the representative for a party in a riding.

canvassing: soliciting votes or memberships. The Canada Elections Act limits door-to-door canvassing to between the hours of 9:00 a.m. and 9:00 p.m. Provincial and Municipal Elections Acts may have different rights and rules for candidates.

caucus: a group of similar politicians, often from the same party (e.g., the Liberal caucus) or with shared interests or locations (e.g., women's caucus, regional caucus).

Centre Block: the main building on Parliament Hill in Ottawa, which houses the House of Commons and Senate chambers. It is currently under construction for an estimated ten-year renovation.

Chief: There are two types of Chiefs: a Band Chief and a Hereditary Chief. Under the Indian Act, a Band Chief is elected every two years by band members, whereas the leadership of a Hereditary Chief is passed down through generations or through other cultural protocols.

Confederation: Canada became a country, the Dominion of Canada, in 1867. Beginning in 1864, colonial politicians — the Fathers of Confederation — negotiated the creation of a constitution for a new country, resulting in the British North America (BNA) Act, which is Canada's Constitution, enacted by the British Parliament. At its creation in 1867, the Dominion of Canada included four provinces: Nova Scotia, New Brunswick, Quebec, and Ontario. Between then and 1999, six more provinces and three territories joined Confederation.

contestant: a person who wants to be named the official candidate for a political party in an electoral district. A successful contestant becomes a candidate.

crossing the floor: when a sitting politician of a party leaves to join a different party.

Deputy Leader: the second-in-command of a political party, after the party leader.

electoral reform/democratic reform: the process of changing electoral, or voting, systems. Canada follows a "first-past-the-post" voting system: Canadians cast one single vote, and the candidate with the most votes wins. The elected representative does not have to have a majority of the votes; the elected winner in a riding with three or more candidates may receive less than 50% of the vote. Alternative voting systems include preferential balloting and proportional representation.

electoral system: Canada's electoral system is a single-member plurality, also known as a plurality electoral system, or a first-past-the-post system. In every electoral district, the candidate with the highest number of votes wins a seat as that riding's member of Parliament or member of the legislature. Under this electoral system, a majority of voters may not have voted for the candidate elected. Other electoral systems include majority systems, proportional representation systems, and mixed electoral systems. Examples of majority systems include alternative vote (or preferential balloting) and run-off (or two-round) systems, designed to elect the person with the majority of the votes. Proportional representation systems aim to match a party's vote share with its representation in the legislature. Examples of proportional representation systems include single transferable vote and list proportional representation. Lastly, mixed electoral systems create different combinations of the electoral systems outlined above.

First Nations sovereignty: the power or authority of a state to govern itself and its subjects, and First Nations' right to self-determination, including the need for the Canadian government to work with First Nations on a nation-to-nation or government-to-government basis.

G7: a consensus-based forum of seven countries: Canada, France, Germany, Italy, Japan, the United Kingdom, and the United States. The G7 works together on gender equality, climate change, and more.

GBA+: a public policy tool that enables decision-makers to see the impact of their proposals on the lives of people of all genders and intersections of identity.

GRB: a public policy tool that seeks to ensure that budgets benefit the whole of society. The tool addresses the collection and allocation of public resources to ensure that the resources contribute to advancing gender equality and women's empowerment.

House Leader: Each recognized party — a party with at least 12 MPs in the House of Commons — appoints one member to be its House Leader. The House Leaders meet regularly to set agendas and hold negotiations.

House of Commons: The House of Commons is made up of the elected members of Parliament (MPs) and is one of the three parts of Parliament, along with the unelected Senate and the appointed Governor General (the representative of the Crown).

Indian Act: Passed in 1876, the Indian Act is a piece of federal legislation that regulates "Indians" — First Nations peoples — through status, government, and resources.

Indigenous hereditary and elected leadership: two different types of Indigenous governing structures. Elected leaders — Chiefs and Band Councils — operate under a governing structure that was imposed by the Canadian federal government through the Indian Act. Hereditary leaderships span generations of families. These different governance systems are not universally recognized by all Indigenous peoples.

Inter-Parliamentary Union: an international organization that works toward building global democracy and includes participation from 178 parliaments, including Canada.

Legislative Assembly: a body of people elected in a province or territory to create and pass laws.

minister: a member of cabinet. See "cabinet."

motion vs bill: a motion is a formal proposal representative of public interest and is used to attract attention to social and political issues. A bill is a draft of a proposed law.

MP: member of Parliament. A national election, sometimes called a federal election or a Canadian general election, is an election to pick the members of the House of Commons; an individual member is known as a member of Parliament (MP).

MHA, MLA, MNA, MPP: a person who is a member of a legislative body for a province or territory. The names of legislative bodies may differ depending on the province or territory.

MHA: a member of the House of Assembly in Newfoundland and Labrador.

MLA: a member of the Legislative Assembly in Alberta, British Columbia, Manitoba, New Brunswick, Northwest Territories, Nova Scotia, Nunavut, Prince Edward Island, Saskatchewan, or Yukon.

MNA: a member of the National Assembly in Quebec.

MPP: a member of the provincial Parliament in Ontario.

municipal councillor (also city councillor): a municipal representative of constituents of a ward on city council; councillors do not usually run for election under a party's banner but rather run as independents.

name on the ballot (NOB) (also paper candidate): In elections, political parties try to have a candidate in every riding in order to promote a strong presence across the province or country. In ridings where the party might never have won, no one may present for the nomination. In these cases, the party may resort to asking people to be a "name on the ballot" (NOB), or a "paper candidate."

NGO: a non-governmental organization (not related to government) that generally addresses a social or political issue.

Official Opposition: the party with the second-largest number of seats in the House of Commons. The Leader of the Opposition must be consulted before decisions are made, and the leader's role is to challenge and hold the government in power accountable.

preferential balloting: a system that asks voters to rank the candidates in order of preference on their ballot. If nobody wins a simple majority outright, the person with the least number of votes drops off, and this candidate's second-place votes are distributed to other candidates. This cycle continues until someone accumulates more than 50 percent of the vote. Preferential balloting is used during nomination meetings in order to declare a candidate.

school board trustee: A school board trustee is elected as a member of a municipal school board every four years during a municipal election. A trustee represents a community's concerns, values, needs, and expectations.

Senate: Senators are appointed by the governor general on the advice of the prime minister and may hold their positions until age 75. After the House of Commons passes a bill, the bill must also pass a vote in the Senate before it becomes law.

Speaker (of the House): The Speaker is appointed to maintain order in the House of Commons and to guide the House through daily agendas. The Speaker does not participate in debates and casts a vote only in the case of a tie.

Truth and Reconciliation Commission (TRC): The TRC was launched in 2008 as part of the Indian Residential Schools Settlement Agreement (IRSSA) to facilitate reconciliation among former students along with their families and communities.

REFERENCES

PREAMBLE

Canadian Charter of Rights and Freedoms, s 15, Part 1 of the *Constitution Act, 1982*, being Schedule B to the *Canada Act 1982* (UK), 1982, c 11.

Historica Canada. (n.d.) *Women's suffrage in Canada education guide* [Data file]. Retrieved from http://education.historicacanada.ca/files/108/Womens_Suffrage.pdf

Inter-Parliamentary Union. (2019). [Map that captures women's participation in executive government and in parliament on 1 January 2019.] *Women in politics: 2019.* Retrieved from https://www.ipu.org/resources/publications/infographics/2019-03/women-in-politics-2019

Woetzel, J., Madgavkar, A., Ellingrud, K., Labaye, E., Devillard, S., Kutcher, E. … Krishnan, M. (2015). How advancing women's equality can add $12 trillion to global growth. Retrieved from https://www.mckinsey.com/featured-insights/employment-and-growth/how-advancing-womens-equality-can-add-12-trillion-to-global-growth

World Economic Forum. (2016). The case for gender parity. Retrieved from http://reports.weforum.org/global-gender-gap-report-2016/the-case-for-gender-parity/

PART 1 ASSESSING THE JOURNEY

Introduction

Canadian Women's Foundation. (2017). Fact sheet moving women into leadership [PDF file]. Retrieved from https://www.canadianwomen.org/wp-content/uploads/2017/09/Facts-About-Women-and-Leadership.pdf

Inter-Parliamentary Union. (2019). *Women in national parliaments* [Data file]. Retrieved from http://archive.ipu.org/wmn-e/arc/classif010119.htm

Loprespub (2015). Women in Canada's Parliament. Retrieved from https://hillnotes.ca/2015/11/04/women-in-canadas-parliament-making-progress-2/

Statistics Canada. (2015). *Total population, Canada, 1921 to 2061* [Data file]. Retrieved from https://www150.statcan.gc.ca/n1/pub/89-503-x/2010001/article/11475/tbl/tbl001-eng.htm

Toward Parity in Municipal Politics. (n.d.). Retrieved from https://fcm.ca/en/programs/women-in-local-government/toward-parity-in-municipal-politics

Tremblay, M., & Trimble, L. (2005). Representation of Canadian women at the cabinet table. *Atlantis: Critical Studies in Gender, Culture & Social Justice, 30*(1). Retrieved from https://era.library.ualberta.ca/items/b3c571d7-3c45-4784-858c-8bb5eeee397c/view/f5b17a71-5563-471f-8b6b-00117e971ae0/857-1110-1-PB.pdf

Changing the Political Landscape

Statistics Canada. (2013). *Canada's total population estimates, 2013* [Data file]. Statistics Canada catalogue no. 11-001-X. Retrieved from https://www150.statcan.gc.ca/n1/en/daily-quotidien/130926/dq130926a-eng.pdf?st=s2gsJkED

Politics and Identity

Crenshaw, C. (1989). Demarginalizing the intersection of race and sex: A Black feminist critique of antidiscrimination doctrine, feminist theory and antiracist politics. *University of Chicago Legal Forum 1989*(1). Retrieved from http://chicagounbound.uchicago.edu/uclf/vol1989/iss1/8

Runyan, A. S. (2018). What is intersectionality and why is it important? Retrieved from https://www.aaup.org/article/what-intersectionality-and-why-it-important#.XK30j5NKhBx

Run, Ask, or Support

Heard, A. (2011). *Women candidates, Canadian federal elections, 1921-2011* [Data file]. Retrieved from https://www.sfu.ca/~aheard/elections/women-elected.html

United Nations Division for the Advancement of Women (DAW). Equal participation of women and men in decision-making processes, with particular emphasis on political participation and leadership [PDF file]. (2005). Retrieved from https://www.un.org/womenwatch/daw/egm/eql-men/FinalReport.pdf

PART 2 WHAT DOES IT TAKE?

Getting on the Ballot

Cowper-Smith, Y., Kopec, A., Sutton, T., & Nelson, K. (2017). Women and politics: Overcoming barriers to participation in leadership [PDF file]. Retrieved from https://atrium.lib.uoguelph.ca/xmlui/bitstream/handle/10214/10505/CowperSmith_etal_WomenAndPolitics_AODA.pdf?sequence=4

Equal Voice. (2018). Getting to the gate: Discover your pathway to find success in politics. Retrieved from https://d3n8a8pro7vhmx.cloudfront.net/equalvoice/pages/67/attachments/original/1541617153/Getting-to-the_Gate_Guidebook_2018-EN.pdf?1541617153

Wicks, A., & Lang-Dion, R. (2007). *Equal Voice: Electing more women in Canada* [PDF file]. Retrieved from http://www.revparl. ca/30/1/30n1_07e_wicks-lang-dion.pdf

PART 3 HOW TO SURVIVE — AND THRIVE

Introduction

Geiger, A., & Kent, L. (2017). Number of women leaders around the world has grown, but they're still a small group. Retrieved from https://www.pewresearch.org/fact-tank/2017/03/08/women-leaders-around-the-world/

World Economic Forum. (2017). *The global gender gap report 2017* [PDF File]. Retrieved from http://www3.weforum.org/docs/WEF_GGGR_2017.pdf

Managing the Message

D'Arcy, P. (2017, Aug 11). Why freedom of the press is more important now than ever. Retrieved from https://ideas.ted.com/why-freedom-of-the-press-is-more-important-now-than-ever/

Finding the Money

Canadian Women's Foundation. (2018). The facts about the gender wage gap in Canada. Retrieved from https://www.canadianwomen.org/the-facts/the-wage-gap/

McIntyre, C. (2018, Feb 8). Why do men make more money than women? Retrieved from https://www.macleans.ca/society/why-do-men-make-more-money-than-women/

Napolitano, J. (2018, Sept 4). Women earn more college degrees and men still earn more money. Retrieved from https://www.forbes.com/sites/janetnapolitano/2018/09/04/women-earn-more-college-degrees-and-men-still-earn-more-money/#2c99aa3439f1

Complex Trade-Offs

Correll, S., Benard, S., & Paik, I. (2007). Getting a job: Is there a motherhood penalty? *American Journal of Sociology, 112*(5). Retrieved from http://www.jstor.org/stable/10.1086/511799

Kaplan, S. (2018, Sept 25). The motherhood penalty. Retrieved from https://magazine.utoronto.ca/opinion/the-motherhood-penalty-gender-wage-gap-sarah-kaplan/

Miller, C. C. (2014, Sept 6). The motherhood penalty vs. the fatherhood bonus. Retrieved from https://www.nytimes.com/2014/09/07/upshot/a-child-helps-your-career-if-youre-a-man.html

PART 4 A WORLD MADE ANEW

Making Herstory Visible

Historica Canada. (n.d.) Women in Canadian history education guide [PDF file]. Retrieved from https://tce-live2.s3.amazonaws.com/media/education_guides/english_guides/Women-In-Canadian-History-Education-Guide-single%20pages.pdf

Statistics Canada. (2017, Oct 25). Aboriginal peoples in Canada: Key results from the 2016 Census. Retrieved from https://www150.statcan.gc.ca/n1/daily-quotidien/171025/dq171025a-eng.htm

Statistics Canada. (2017, Nov 29). Education in Canada: Key results from the 2016 Census. Retrieved from https://www150.statcan.gc.ca/n1/daily-quotidien/171129/dq171129a-eng.htm

Universities Canada. (n.d.). Facts and stats. Retrieved from https://www.univcan.ca/universities/facts-and-stats/

Creating Enduring Change

City of Edmonton. (2018, Apr 12). *Gender-based analysis + : What is it and why?* [Video file]. Retrieved from https://www.youtube.com/watch?v=p6w-d1mmjFU

Government of Canada. (2010). Whole-of-government framework. Retrieved from https://www.canada.ca/en/treasury-board-secretariat/services/reporting-government-spending/whole-government-framework.html

Government of Canada. (2016). Gender-based analysis. Retrieved from https://www.canada.ca/en/treasury-board-secretariat/services/treasury-board-submissions/gender-based-analysis-plus.html

Government of Canada. (2017). Electoral systems factsheet. Retrieved from https://www.canada.ca/en/campaign/electoral-reform/learn-about-canadian-federal-electoral-reform/electoral-systems-factsheet.html

Inter-Parliamentary Union. (2015). [Map that captures women's participation in executive government and in parliament on 1 January 2015]. *Women in politics: 2015*. Retrieved from https://www.ipu.org/resources/publications/infographics/2016-07/women-in-politics-2015

Inter-Parliamentary Union. (2017). [Map that captures women's participation in executive government and in parliament on 1 January 2017]. *Women in politics: 2017*. Retrieved from https://www.ipu.org/resources/publications/infographics/2017-03/women-in-politics-2017

UN Women. (n.d.). Gender responsive budgeting. Retrieved from http://asiapacific.unwomen.org/en/focus-areas/women-poverty-economics/gender-responsive-budgeting

UN Women. (2017, Feb 23). *What is gender responsive budgeting* [Video file]. Retrieved from https://www.youtube.com/watch?v = mquOclPJYPs

More Than Just Numbers

Devillard, S., Vogel, T., Pickersgill, A., Madgavkar, A., Nowski, T., Krishnan, M., ... Kechrid, D. (2017). The power of parity: Advancing women's equality in Canada. Retrieved from https://www.mckinsey.com/featured-insights/gender-equality/the-power-of-parity-advancing-womens-equality-in-canada

UN News. (2018, Oct 25). 'Crippling to our credibility' that number of women peacekeepers is so low: UN chief. Retrieved from https://news.un.org/en/story/2018/10/1024122

POSTSCRIPT: THAT'S IT! I'M RUNNING!

Chozick, A. (2015, Sept 5). Hillary Clinton's Beijing speech on women resonates 20 years later. Retrieved from https://www.nytimes.com/politics/first-draft/2015/09/05/20-years-later-hillary-clintons-beijing-speech-on-women-resonates/

Government of Canada. (2018). Women and climate change. Retrieved from https://www.canada.ca/en/environment-climate-change/services/climate-change/women.html

The Climate Reality Project. (2018). How is climate change affecting women? Retrieved from https://www.climaterealityproject.org/blog/how-climate-change-affecting-women

United Nations. (1996). Report of the fourth world conference on women [PDF file]. Retrieved from https://www.un.org/womenwatch/daw/beijing/pdf/Beijing%20full%20report%20E.pdf

INDEX

Aariak, Eva, 16–17, 32, 207
AFN Women's Council, 40, 193, 224
Akapo, Kemi, 59
Archibald, RoseAnne, 40–41, 139, 173
Ashton, Niki, 100, 102–103, 121–122, 144, 188–189
Augustine, Jean, 24–25, 126, 194

Bakopanos, Eleni, 161
Beaudry-Mellor, Tina, 72, 162, 191
Beijing Fourth World Conference on Women, 43, 184, 194, 214
Bennett, Carolyn, 38, 123, 194
Benson, Sheri, 39, 57–58, 78–79
Bergen, Candice, 58, 120–121
Bernard, Joanne, 122–123, 203
Biondi, Yvette, 95–96
Bokhari, Rana, 49, 129, 138
Brosseau, Ruth Ellen, 85, 176

Caesar-Chavannes, Celina, 20, 48, 170–171
Campbell, Kim, 17–20, 115, 198–199, 216
Canada Elections Act, 12, 65, 67, 76, 133, 200, 226, 233
Canadian Charter of Rights and Freedoms, 53, 184, 233
Canadian Human Rights Act, 56, 133, 226, 231–232
Canadian Labour Congress (CLC), 69, 156, 224
Carney, Pat, 97, 183
Chagger, Bardish, 33–34
Chau, Jeannette, 83
Chow, Olivia, 210–211
Clancy, Mary, 164–165
Cochrane, Caroline, 134–135
Copps, Sheila, 34, 181–182
Crombie, Bonnie, 151

Daughters of the Vote, 176, 224
Davies, Libby, 37, 63, 112, 117, 139, 156, 160
Dhillon, Anju, 43–44
DiNovo, Cheri, 28, 60, 154–155, 228
Duncan, Linda, 92, 191

Equal Voice, 52, 63, 66, 72, 174, 176, 191, 217, 224

Famous Five, 13, 182
Federation of Canadian Municipalities (FCM), 72, 224

Fife, Catherine, 60, 70, 186
Fontaine, Nahanni, 21–22, 129, 192, 230
Fry, Hedy, 56–57, 140–141, 194

Ganley, Rosemary, 142, 216
gender-based analysis plus (GBA+), 173, 184, 186, 193, 234
Gender Equality Advisory Council, 142, 194, 200–201
gender responsive budgeting (GRB), 173, 193, 234
Grey, Deb, 62–63, 166–167

Hollett, Jennifer, 158–159
Horwath, Andrea, 60–61, 199, 202
Hughes, Carol, 69, 156

iKNOW Politics, 71, 225
Indian Act, 12, 233, 235

Jaczek, Helena, 81
Jansen, Sandra, 117, 123–124
Jaquays, Cammie, 167–168, 217
Jennings, Marlene, 50
Jinkerson, Barb, 94
Jones, Yvonne, 89

Khalid, Iqra, 74, 117–119, 226
Khan, Farheen, 23, 45, 185
Kwan, Jenny, 28–29, 125

LaRocca, Kelly, 110–111
Lathlin, Amanda, 35–36, 178–179
Levis, Kara, 68–69

MacCharles, Tracy, 82
MacDonald, Flora, 212–213
Maghnam, Stephanie, 72–73
Matthews, Deb, 208
May, Elizabeth, 34–35, 66, 90–91, 100, 106–107, 152, 173, 179–180
McCallion, Hazel, 30–31, 139, 151, 184
McCrimmon, Karen, 41, 73, 100, 103–104, 149, 211
McDonough, Alexa, 34, 70–71, 136–137, 164, 177, 205, 210
McGregor, Eileen "Stevie," 7, 56
McKenna, Catherine, 88, 153
McLaughlin, Audrey, 34, 55, 107, 126–127, 136, 196–197
McLellan, Anne, 53, 163–164
McLeod, Lyn, 108, 120, 145
Metcalfe, Isabel, 182
Monsef, Maryam, 80–81, 168, 194
Montufar, Jeannette, 168–169, 209
Murray, Joyce, 109, 195

Naidoo-Harris, Indira, 27, 124–125, 228
Nawaz, Rasheda, 78

Oger, Morgane, 29, 127–128, 187
Opekokew, Delia, 113

Peckford, Nancy, 63, 217
Persons Case, 12
Plante, Valérie, 117, 130–131, 201–202
Pollock, Jennifer, 70–71

Raitt, Lisa, 42, 101–102, 146–147, 190
Regan, Kelly, 52–53, 148
Reid, Linda, 22, 93
Rempel, Michelle, 185–186

Sandill, Shubha, 38
Sarauer, Nicole, 54, 100, 104–105, 190, 229
Sattler, Peggy, 26–27, 60, 87–88, 227
Schulte, Deb, 84, 169
Senis, Sherry, 73–74
Setaram, Sharmila, 99
Slavin, Linda, 92–93, 203–204
Smith, Mary, 165–166
snowflake model, 88–89
Squires, Rochelle, 77, 129, 150
Status of Women, 24, 124, 129, 134, 150, 164, 169, 180, 191, 194
Sutherland, Sylvia, 94

Therrien, Diane, 137
Truth and Reconciliation Commission (TRC), 33, 175, 179, 236

United Nations (UN), 37, 56, 173, 184, 195, 225

Vandenbeld, Anita, 71, 162–163

Watson, Heather, 98, 217
Williams, Phyllis, 32–33, 143, 157
Wilson, Helen, 79
Wynne, Kathleen, 16–17, 46–47, 73, 128, 204

yellow sail, 65, 98
Yip, Jean, 51
YWCA, 59, 70, 72, 225

Zann, Lenore, 132, 180–181
Zippel, Kim, 135–136, 150–151

PHOTO CREDITS

Cover: pattern—maximmmmum/Shutterstock.com; Betsy McGregor—Joe Keenan; 11: Betsy McGregor—Michael Cullen; [13: FamousFive—SBshot87; 14: doors—David P. Lewis] Shutterstock.com; 16: [Alison Redford—Dan Riedlhuber/Reuters; Christy Clark—Ben Nelms/Reuters; Eva Aariak—Chris Wattie/Reuters; Kathy Dunderdale—Greg Locke/Reuters; Pauline Marois—Christinne Muschi/Reuters; Rachel Notley—Dan Riedlhuber/Reuters] Newscom; Kathleen Wynne—Jenna Muirhead for the Ontario Liberal Party; 18: Campbell portrait—Keith Levit/Alamy Stock Photo; 20: Celina Caesar-Chavannes—House of Commons; 21: Nahanni Fontaine—Courtesy of Nahanni Fontaine; 22: Linda Reid—Courtesy of Linda Reid; 23: Farheen Khan—Anurita Mohan; 25: Jean Augustine—Lawrence Kerr Media; 26: Peggy Sattler—Courtesy of Peggy Sattler; 27: Indira Naidoo-Harris—Jenna Muirhead Photography; 28: Cheri DiNovo—Courtesy of Cheri DiNovo; Jenny Kwan—House of Commons; 29: Morgane Oger—Courtesy of Morgane Oger; 31: Hazel McCallion—Helen Sessions/age fotostock/Superstock; 32: Phyllis Williams—Courtesy of Phyllis Williams; 33: Bardish Chagger—House of Commons; 34: Elizabeth May—Courtesy of Elizabeth May; 35: Amanda Lathlin—Tracey Goncalves; 37: Libby Davies—Kim Elliott; 38: Carolyn Bennett—Tom Sandler; Shubha Sandill—Courtesy of Shubha Sandill; 39: Sheri Benson—House of Commons; 40: RoseAnne Archibald—Courtesy of RoseAnne Archibald; 41: Karen McCrimmon—Courtesy of Karen McCrimmon; 42: Lisa Raitt—Chris Wattie/Reuters/Newscom; 43: Anju Dhillon—Courtesy of Anju Dhillon; 46: Kathleen Wynne—Fred Thornhill/Reuters/Newscom; 49: Rana Bokhari—Courtesy of Rana Bokhari; 50: Marlene Jennings—Courtesy of Marlene Jennings; 51: Jean Yip—Courtesy of Jean Yip; 52: Kelly Regan—Sue Siri Photography; 53: Anne McLellan—Darcy Scaife; 54: Nicole Sarauer—Courtesy of Nicole Sarauer; 55: Audrey McLaughlin—Courtesy of Audrey McLaughlin; 56: Hedy Fry—Courtesy of Hedy Fry; 58: Candice Bergen—House of Commons; 59: Kemi Akapo—Kemi Akapo; 61: Andrea Horwath—Courtesy of Andrea Horwath; 62: Deborah Grey—Angela Walker; 63: Nancy Peckford—The Canadian Press/Adrian Wyld; 64: lion—Alexander Sviridov/Shutterstock.com; 66: hallway; Daughters of the Vote; Elizabeth May; Catherine McKenna] Courtesy of Equal Voice; 68: Kara Levis—Jon Yee; 69: Carol Hughes—Courtesy of Carol Hughes; 70: Catherine Fife—Adam Scotti/PMO; Jennifer Pollock—Trudie Lee; 71: Anita Vandenbeld—The Canadian Press/Sean Kilpatrick; 72: Tina Beaudry-Mellor—The Saskatchewan Party; Stephanie Maghnam—Jean-Marc Caraisse; 73: Sherry Senis—Courtesy of Sherry Senis; 74: Iqra Khalid—Irfan Siddiqui; 77: Rochelle Squires—Courtesy of Rochelle Squires; 78: Rasheda Nawaz—Courtesy of Rasheda Nawaz; 79: Helen Wilson—Courtesy of Helen Wilson; 80: Maryam Monsef—Peter Mitchell; 81: Helena Jaczek—Liberal Caucus Services Bureau Queen's Park; 82: Tracy MacCharles—Jenna Muirhead-Gould; 83: Jeannette Chau—Maggie Habieda/Fotografia Boutique; 84: Deb Schulte—Courtesy of Deb Schulte; 85: Ruth Ellen Brosseau—Courtesy of Ruth Ellen Brosseau; 87: [Anna Gainey—John Woods; Jenni Byrne—Jonathan Hayward; Katie Telford—Matthew Usherwood] The Canadian Press; Anne McGrath—IanCapstick; Rebecca Blaikie—Joel Duff, OFL Communications Department; 88: Catherine McKenna—Adam Scotti/House of Commons; 89: Yvonne Jones—Courtesy of Yvonne Jones; 92: Linda Duncan—Courtesy of Linda Duncan; Linda Slavin—Courtesy of Linda Slavin; 94: Barb Jinkerson—Courtesy of Barb Jinkerson; Sylvia Sutherland—Michelle Sutherland; 95: Yvette Biondi—Courtesy of Yvette Biondi; 96: Pat Carney—Nancy Angermeyer Photography; 98: Heather Watson—Courtesy of Heather Watson; 99: Sharmila Setaram—Rose Ha; 102: Niki Ashton—Asclepias; 108: Lyn McLeod—Courtesy of Lyn McLeod; 109: Joyce Murray—Courtesy of Joyce Murray; 111: Kelly LaRocca—Courtesy of Kelly LaRocca; 113: Delia Opekokew—Courtesy of Delia Opekokew; 114: House of Commons interior—Wangkun Jia/Shutterstock.com; 116: cameras—microgen/iStock.com; 122: Joanne Bernard—Courtesy of Joanne Bernard; 123: Sandra Jansen—Courtesy of Sandra Jansen; 131: Valerie Plante—Martin Girard/shootstudio.ca; 132: Lenore Zann—Courtesy of Lenore Zann; 134: Caroline Cochrane—Courtesy of Caroline Cochrane; 135: Kim Zippel—Courtesy of Kim Zippel; 136: Alexa McDonough—iPhoto Inc./Newscom; 137: Diane Therrien—Lance Anderson/Peterborough This Week; 142: Rosemary Ganley—Courtesy of Rosemary Ganley; 147: Lisa Raitt—Chris Wattie/Reuters/Newscom; 151: Bonnie Crombie—City of Mississauga; 158: Jennifer Hollett—Jessica Laforet; 161: Eleni Bakopanos—Gaëlle Vuillaume; 164: Mary Clancy—CP Photo/Andrew Vaughan; 165: Mary Smith—Rebekah Littlejohn Photography; 167: Cammie Jaquays—Courtesy of Cammie Jaquays; 168: Jeannette Montufar—Credit Rollan Temporosa; 172: clock tower—Joyce Nelson/Shutterstock.com; 174: Daughters of the Vote—Chris Wattie/Reuters/Newscom; 181: Sheila Copps—Blair Gable/Reuters/Newscom; 182: Isabel Metcalfe—Couvrette Photography; 185: Michelle Rempel—Andrew Scheer; 198: Kim Campbell—Simon Fraser University-University Communications/CC; 208: Deb Matthews—Courtesy of Deb Matthews; 210: Olivia Chow—Fred Thornhill/Reuters/Newscom; 213: Flora MacDonald—Keystone Press/Alamy